THE PSYCHOLOGICAL TOOLKIT

Jennifer Evans Fitzsimons

THE PSYCHOLOGICAL TOOLKIT

A Workbook for a
Positive Self and Identity

ROBINSON

ROBINSON

First published in Great Britain in 2023 by Robinson

1 3 5 7 9 10 8 6 4 2

Copyright © Jennifer Evans Fitzsimons, 2023
Illustrations by Phoebe Munday

The moral right of the author has been asserted.

A CIP catalogue record for this book
is available from the British Library.

ISBN: 978-1-47214-712-7

Typeset in Palatino by Initial Typesetting Services, Edinburgh
Printed and bound in Great Britain by Bell and Bain Ltd, Glasgow

Papers used by Robinson are from well-managed forests and other responsible sources.

Robinson
An imprint of
Little, Brown Book Group
Carmelite House
50 Victoria Embankment
London EC4Y 0DZ

An Hachette UK Company
www.hachette.co.uk

www.littlebrown.co.uk

To Matthew, my husband and best friend.

To our five wonderful children, Clara, Maitiú, Oscar, Dáire and Rossa.

*You are all the **Loves** of my life!*

Contents

Part 3
Using My Psychological Toolkit

Welcome

The way you think about yourself affects how you live your life!

Welcome to *The Psychological Toolkit*, where you will learn how to use psychology to help you on your journey to knowing your true self. Throughout this workbook, you will see that how you communicate with yourself and make meaning about yourself has an impact on your psychological health. As Elkhonon Goldberg so rightly claimed, our success in life depends on our capacity for insight into our own mental world.[1] As you progress through this self-development workbook, you will begin to understand that your most important relationship is the one that you have with yourself.

Throughout the following chapters, I will guide you through the development of your own positive theory and view of your unique self and identity. For some this will be a new path to self-discovery, for others it may be a rediscovery of a more positive way of thinking. What this means is that you will learn how to think on a deeper level about yourself, through honest, non-judgemental questioning.

Why should you read and complete this workbook?

- Do you want to develop a positive view of yourself, and engage proactively with the world and those around you?

- Do you want to develop thinking skills and the necessary psychological tools and resources to develop and maintain your own positive sense of self and identity?

- Do you want to develop a strong understanding of your own self and identity, and your ongoing story of yourself?

- Do you want to improve your autonomy and ability to shape your own theory of self and identity, to take power over and ownership of your own thoughts, feelings and behaviours?

- Do you want to take more control of your wellbeing, resilience and mental health?

- Do you want to experience increases in your self-esteem and your self-awareness?

- Do you want to improve your pro-social and citizenship behaviours, to make a more positive impact in the world?

- Do you want to connect to your inner voice and to become your own personal advisor?

Have you been answering YES to these questions? Then this workbook is for you!

Self-work and psychology

The thoughts, values and ideas you have about yourself are your own creation and are owned by you. You, therefore, have full rights to change and develop them as you see fit. Self-work activities are the sense-making processes that provide a toolkit for how you think about yourself, in order to understand, make meaning of, and manage:

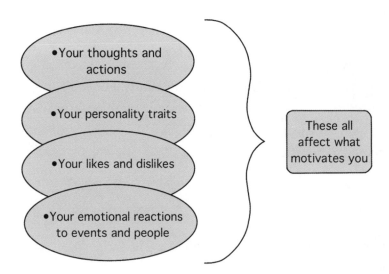

Therefore, self-work provides you with the psychological resources to develop and maintain a positive self and identity.

The field of psychology is useful for exploring and applying self-work to your life, to improve your sense of self and wellbeing.

- The field of *psychology* is the scientific study of how our mind works and how it affects our behaviour. The focus is on understanding why we do what we do. (We will return to the topic of scientific study later in this chapter.)

- *Psychological* means something that occurs in your mind. We use the term for things that occur internally in us. For example, our thoughts and emotions.

- It can also refer to something that is related to psychology, for example 'psychological terms' refer to terms that are related to psychology.

- The field of *positive psychology* focuses on our strengths and abilities, on positive emotions and on how the self can act as a gatekeeper of negative emotions.

- Psychological resources are internal skills which help us to satisfy our needs, wants and goals. They are like a psychological toolkit drawn upon to improve our self-worth and maintain positive self and identity.

'I am the mind, and the mind is I'
– Chan, 2008[2]

'Minds are what brains do'
– Minsky, 1986[3]

It will become very apparent to you that self-work is a deliberate (rather than a passive, hit-or-miss) type of thinking. It is quite similar to a quality control system, involving planning, monitoring and evaluating your thinking and reasoning. Another important feature involves keeping your negative thoughts in check and promoting your positive ones.

These features of our self-work processing are involved in what's called metacognition, which we will work on in Chapter 2.

We will also practise self-work activities for self-improvement. This is self-improvement by *your* standards and values, with the primary aim of improving your psychological wellbeing and your positive sense of self.

Off the top of your head, think of one thing that you would like to improve about how you think about yourself.

_____

_____

_____

_____

_____

_____

_____

_____

_____

_____

As you progress through the self-work activities in this workbook, you will develop a very effective toolkit for improving how you view yourself.

You can return to what you have written later on, to see how your thinking and meaning-making have developed.

Think of five values that you have that you believe are important in the way you live your life.

1. _____

2. _____

3. _____

4. _____

5. _____

The importance of your values to your meaning-making will become clear as you progress through this workbook.

Take a moment and think of two people (A and B) that you think are just the most confident and successful people that you know, and fill in below:

Confident and successful person A: _____

Describe this person in one sentence:

_____

_____

Confident and successful person B: _____

Describe this person in one sentence:

_____

_____

Rest assured that the two people on your list already practise self-work, which is to say they take the time to carry out self-work activities and continually make meaning of their self and identity. You will see that managing the self is an important behind-the-scenes function. Persons A and B from your list certainly take the time to manage themselves and to find clarity, which helps them to make better choices.

Are there any similarities between A and B and you?

The following questionnaire gives an initial assessment of your ability to make sense of how you think and make meaning about yourself. This is a very useful exercise to carry out before you read and complete this workbook. It allows you to get an idea of where you place yourself, so that you can see the gains achieved in your meaning-making and sense-making as you progress and become more insightful.

Initial evaluation of your sense-making skills

The following statements are based on how you generally feel about your sense-making skills. Read through the following state-ments and, for each item, select one of the response choices, and write the number for your choice in the space provided. Remember to answer as honestly and accurately as you can.

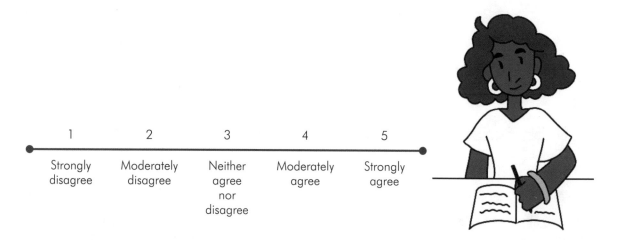

1	2	3	4	5
Strongly disagree	Moderately disagree	Neither agree nor disagree	Moderately agree	Strongly agree

1. I often think about my thoughts and feelings   _____

2. I usually know how I really feel about things   _____

3. I often think about why I behave the way I do   _____

4. I often try to make sense of my behaviour   _____

5. I often try to understand how my thoughts and feelings emerge   _____

6. I am very aware of my thoughts and feelings   _____

7. I usually understand why I behave in certain ways   _____

8. I am rarely confused by my own behaviour   _____

9. I know what type of person I am   _____

10. I generally have a good idea about why I behaved in a certain way   _____

Total score   _____

Interpreting your results

10   20   30   40   50

Low evaluation of your sense-making skills   High evaluation of your sense-making skills

Reflecting on your initial evaluation

Have you evaluated your sense-making skills as high, moderate or low?

Are you surprised by your evaluation?

Do you think that your sense-making skills could be improved?

The scientific field of psychology

Before I had my children, I lectured in psychology in Dublin for many years. During this time, one of the areas I lectured in was research and experimental design in psychology, at both undergraduate and postgraduate level.

What is science?

When you think of the word 'science', what is the first image that comes to mind?

_____

_____

_____

This is a question I always asked at the beginning of research methods classes. Answers would range from 'test tubes' and 'computers' to 'investigators in white laboratory coats' and 'new drugs and vaccines'. However, these are not the answer!

Some sciences, such as physics and chemistry, deal with the physical world of electricity and chemicals, etc. These are part of the natural or 'hard sciences', and produce new technologies, which can receive a lot of publicity.

The social and behavioural sciences, such as psychology and sociology, involve the study of people; including their beliefs, attitudes and behaviours. People do not always associate these disciplines with the word 'science', and they are often referred to as 'soft sciences'.

The reference to soft, however, does not mean that the social and behavioural sciences lack scientific rigour, or that they are sloppy or limp. Soft refers to the subject matter. Human behaviour and social life are far more fluid and transient than the tangible elements of chemistry and physics. The natural sciences are not made more scientific than psychology by virtue of their laboratory equipment.[4]

It is important to note that although many processes of inquiry do produce scientific tools and products, the essence of science is the actual process of inquiry.

Very simply, at the essential core of science, we develop questions and find the answers through investigation. Throughout the self-work activities that you will carry out in this workbook, you will ask yourself questions, the answers to which will be part of your positive self-discovery and development.

Ernest Hemingway noted that all you have to do is write one true sentence; the truest sentence that you know.[5] However, this is not as easy as it initially seems. Sometimes it can be difficult to answer questions honestly, in a way that is true to yourself. All sorts of social influences, from group memberships and roles to perceived expectations from significant others, can interfere with your authenticity as a person.

> What would my parents think?
>
> Will my best friend be angry with me?
>
> Who am I going to upset?

As you develop your self-work skills, you will be more mindful of these influences and will be able to process your feelings and actions in an insightful way.

During my years as a lecturer in psychology, I supervised many undergraduate psychology thesis projects. I was always interested in how students developed their questions and the journey they embarked on to answer them. Here you are focusing on the thesis of your sense of self and identity; on your journey to psychological wellbeing. You are asking questions about and finding answers to who you are; adding to your own knowledge base about yourself.

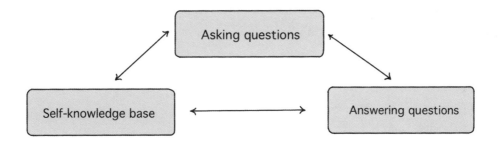

In developing your theory of who you are, or your thesis of your self and identity, the purpose is to help explain and understand your own thoughts, behaviours and desires. Therefore, this is not a theoretical exercise in thought; it must be useful and serve a purpose. As Kurt Lewin so rightly put it, there is nothing as practical as a good theory.[6] It must answer the question WHO AM I? and help you to understand and make sense of your past actions, as well as help you plan for your future.

Psychological terminology and concepts

Science has its own scientific language, which is used by scientists while conducting research, carrying out experiments and when communicating with each other. The same is true in the field of psychology. We use psychological terms, and for some of you, this may be the first time you have been exposed to them.

If this is the case, don't worry, these terms will be explained to you throughout this workbook. In no time at all, you will become comfortable and fluent in using the psychological language of self and identity to describe, explain and understand your unique self.

Ludwig Wittgenstein proposed that the limits of our language are the limits of our world.[7] As you progress through this workbook and learn how to use new psychological terminology, you are in fact opening up a new world of language and understanding for yourself. You will find new ways to understand and describe yourself, and you will broaden your knowledge base.

There is another point to make here. Often these psychological terms are closely related, and the explanations may be quite similar. This unfortunately is an artefact (human made) of all scientific study across the social and behavioural sciences. Within the field of psychology, we often refer to this as conceptual or terminology clutter. We get cluttered with numerous terms that describe the same thing. This is not something to be concerned too much about, and psychological jargon should not intimidate you; my intention is that you can use these terms to describe and make your own sense of your self and identity in an empowering way. You will soon be a fluent user of them.

These terms are worthwhile and of value if we can apply them to our everyday lives. For that to happen, they must allow us to explain, describe and understand our thoughts and behaviours.

 Do not worry about memorising the definitions and descriptions presented throughout. I suggest that you get an intuitive sense or feeling for what the terms mean when you apply them to yourself. If they can aid you in how you can make meaning of who you are and who you want to be, and of your own sense of identity, then I believe that they are doing their job.

More about this workbook

Self-work and using your positivity workbook

While engaging in the self-work activities throughout this workbook, you are making meaning **about you, by you, for you**. You will learn to use strategies to become more self-aware, and to help you reflect on your personality traits, your strengths and abilities, accomplishments, and your motivations.

Many of the self-work activities use journalling, which is a very effective way to develop your meaning-making skills. By telling and writing your story, you begin to understand that who you are emerges from the story you tell of yourself. *Who you actually are is in the telling of your story.*

Of course this constructive and creative process is carried out by all of us, all the time, but we don't always understand its significance. We can use this process to develop a more positive sense of self, and it can help us to plan to self-improve and to set out new goals. This important focus on your ongoing story improves your understanding of your biography, of your inner voice.

The self-journalling, self-reflection and self-work activities presented throughout this workbook will help you to develop your theory of yourself. Once you have written an entry or completed a task, you then have something concrete and tangible to refer back to at any time. For example, you might answer these questions again in a few years' time, and look to see how you have grown and developed.

Maybe during a time when you feel disheartened by an event, or you simply feel a bit low or down in the dumps, you can look back on a very positive entry to remind yourself of your unique strengths. This reminder can help you reframe your thoughts more positively and improve your mood and wellbeing. Cognitively restructure your thoughts!

Before journalling | During journalling | After journalling

Another important benefit of the self-work journal is that completing the activities helps you to see if you do in fact understand the concepts introduced. You get to practise thinking about yourself in the ways suggested, and to ensure that you can apply the concepts. You also have an opportunity to see how your thinking and metacognitive skills have developed.

It also provides you with something tangible: you will have an organised written record of how you describe and understand yourself; your own biography. Remember, you are under no obligation to show anyone your self-work; this is your own personal meaning-making, where you can be as true to yourself as you possibly can. True to your inner voice, your inner story.

You will also:

- have the opportunity to represent your thinking graphically, by filling in diagrams and models in your development of who you are;

- have opportunities to fill out some self-rating questionnaires on different elements of your self-work;

- answer many questions that challenge you and set you in the right direction with your thinking – remember our link between asking questions and science;

- be presented with numerous examples, some from my own personal experiences, others from past clients and friends, which illustrate and illuminate important aspects of self and meaning-making;

- come across illustrative quotes from prominent thinkers covering diverse fields, from artificial intelligence to developmental psychology to cognitive neuroscience to literature;

- find links to YouTube videos and TED Talks (which I have my daughter, Clara, to thank for introducing me to).

Structure of the book

Part 1: Building My Psychological Toolkit

Part 2: A Closer Look at My Social Identity Needs

Part 3: Using My Psychological Toolkit

PART 1

BUILDING MY PSYCHOLOGICAL TOOLKIT

The aim of Part 1 of *The Psychological Toolkit* is to highlight and demonstrate the importance of spending time making sense of yourself, and to equip you with the necessary psychological tools to improve your sense of self and identity.

1 What Does it Mean to Be Me?

Think about this for a moment: the self is at the centre of all of our thoughts!

Well, of course this is the case. Put simply, *you* are the focus of what you think about.

We all know what the self is, we all use the term all the time; we have a sense of ourselves, we refer to ourselves, we talk about ourselves in conversations, and of course we judge ourselves.

As you experience your ongoing sense of who you are, it is important to take the time to find clarity and to understand your meaning-making. Remember that the most important project that you will ever work on is **YOU.**

In this chapter, you are going to:

- develop your thinking skills, to help you to know and understand who you are;

- learn some new psychological terms to use when making sense of who you are;

- consider the significance of your name as an identity marker;

- construct your first set of identity statements.

WHAT DOES IT MEAN TO BE ME?

Before we go any further, have a look at the questions below. Don't worry if this is difficult, or if you cannot think of much to write; just jot down what comes to mind. This is the beginning of your journey and, as you progress through this book, you will find that your answers will become more detailed, and you will have gained more self-understanding.

Who am I?

_____

_____

What does it mean to be a person?

_____

_____

How do I come to know myself?

_____

_____

Am I a good person?

_____

_____

What do I want to do with my life?

_____

_____

Am I capable of change?

_____

_____

What makes me ME, and you YOU?

_____

_____

Answering questions such as those above involves making sense of and finding meaning around what it is to be **'ME'**. This is, of course, your own construction; your own set of ideas and conceptions about your **'SELF'**. As we have discussed in the Welcome chapter, a key self-work activity is _meaning-making_, which involves better understanding your sense of self and identity.

The self is a psychological system – a mental construction that we develop in our minds. In developing your psychological toolkit you will understand the roles played by your cognitive processes, your affective and emotional processes, and your social interaction processes.

The self and identity

Below is an illustration of the psychological system of how we think about ourselves:

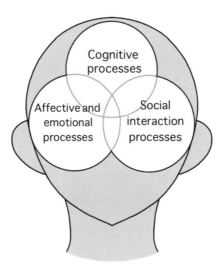

As I mentioned earlier, at such an early point in this workbook, you may be overwhelmed and struggling to answer the questions already presented in this chapter in a way that satisfies you. Please do not be disappointed.

There will also be times when answers are close to hand, and it is quite easy to make sense of your feelings and behaviours, while other times they may be buried deep within you, and you must carry out more in-depth self-work in order to reach your state of positive wellbeing. This self-workbook will help you develop the skills, questions, ideas and models to facilitate clearer communication with yourself.

> *Self* and *identity* can be thought of as simply all the things that you can truly say about yourself, including beliefs, thoughts, memories, physical traits, personality traits and feelings.

For example:

- *I am confident*

- *I worry about what other people think about me*

- *I sometimes feel useless*

- *I am always trying to grow and improve as a person*

- *I would love to be a teacher*

- *I am a great athlete*

- *I am a talented musician*

- *I pay attention to how my emotions affect how I think and behave*

- *I keep my emotions to myself*

- *I visualise my dreams and work to achieve them*

- *I believe that we should look after our planet*

- *I enjoy helping others*

- *I believe that friendships are important*

- *I am quiet and shy*

- *I am good-looking*

- *I have the latest iPhone*

- *I have lots of friends on Facebook and Snapchat*

You already may have begun to realise that **self and identity** are the answer to the question **'Who am I?'** This is who you are in the present moment – as you can see, the list of personal statements above are all in the present tense.

THE MOST FUNDAMENTAL QUESTION ABOUT BEING HUMAN

What you can see is that when we refer to your 'self and identity' we are referring to your subjective psychological conception of your own self as a person. You may already find that using the psychological terms to think about yourself is becoming easier for you.

Does this apply to me? Read through the list of statements about yourself again, and this time tick which ones apply to you. In your initial read-through, you probably already thought about which ones applied to you and which ones didn't. This is a natural tendency. This time, really focus on which apply to you and think of an example or reason for each of your decisions.

I am confident   Yes ☐ / No ☐
Example or reason:

_____

_____

I worry about what other people think about me   Yes ☐ / No ☐
Example or reason:

_____

_____

I sometimes feel useless   Yes ☐ / No ☐
Example or reason:

_____

_____

I am always trying to grow and improve as a person   Yes ☐ / No ☐
Example or reason:

_____

_____

I would love to be a teacher   Yes ☐ / No ☐
Example or reason:

_____

_____

I am a great athlete   Yes ☐ / No ☐
Example or reason:

_____

_____

I am a talented musician   Yes ☐ / No ☐

Example or reason:

_____

_____

I pay attention to how my emotions affect how I think and behave   Yes ☐ / No ☐

Example or reason:

_____

_____

I keep my emotions to myself   Yes ☐ / No ☐

Example or reason:

_____

_____

I visualise my dreams and work to achieve them   Yes ☐ / No ☐

Example or reason:

_____

_____

I believe that we should look after our planet   Yes ☐ / No ☐

Example or reason:

_____

_____

I enjoy helping others   Yes ☐ / No ☐

Example or reason:

_____

_____

Some new psychological terms on the phenomenon of self and identity

Empirical – based on observation or experience, e.g. you can see it or feel it.

A *concept* simply refers to an idea, belief or view, or a theory.

Self – what you take yourself to be – is the *empirical* existence or experience of who you are, as perceived by you. The term *self-concept* is used a lot in psychology to describe our concept or idea of the self. This cognitive process involves *reflexive thinking,* which you will come across on numerous occasions as you progress through the following chapters. What this means is that you take yourself both to be the thinker and also the object which your thoughts are about. This is explained in more detail below.

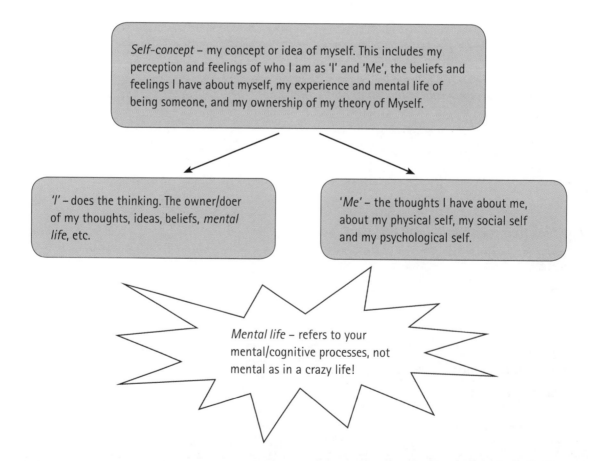

Self-concept – my concept or idea of myself. This includes my perception and feelings of who I am as 'I' and 'Me', the beliefs and feelings I have about myself, my experience and mental life of being someone, and my ownership of my theory of Myself.

'I' – does the thinking. The owner/doer of my thoughts, ideas, beliefs, *mental life*, etc.

'Me' – the thoughts I have about me, about my physical self, my social self and my psychological self.

Mental life – refers to your mental/cognitive processes, not mental as in a crazy life!

It is evident from the diagram that self-concept includes both 'I' and 'Me'. You are a being with a mental life, you are the owner of your subjective experience; of your thoughts, ideas, beliefs, etc.

'I' acts, thinks and carries out activities, for example:	While 'Me' is who we think about, for example:
• I love to paint with watercolours;	• That is **me** in the picture;
• I am feeling sad today;	• That was so unfair to **me**;
• I feel tired after that long walk.	• Who is tired after the walk? **Me**.
(The thinker, the doer, the active agent.)	(Object of the thinking. It's all about me!)

Take some time to think about yourself for a moment, and come up with some examples of **I** and **Me** statements of your own.

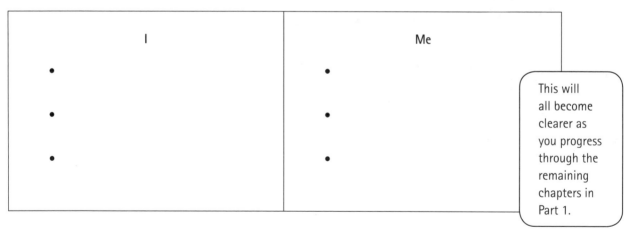

This will all become clearer as you progress through the remaining chapters in Part 1.

- **I** refers to the stream of consciousness inside you.

- **I** is both conscious of your environment, and also conscious of your own existence.

- **I** does the thinking, makes self-awareness and metacognitive work possible.

- **I** fluctuates between different positions and anchor points.

- **I** represents the constant flow of consciousness in your mind, which enables you to become aware of your existence through your experiences.

Myself or me?

It is not unusual for us to misuse the words *me* and *myself*. You may initially think, well, I don't misuse these words, I'm sure I use them all the time when speaking and writing. You might be surprised to learn that you may in fact misuse them on occasion, or even all the time!

Both words are personal pronouns that we use when referring to ourselves. Myself is a *reflexive personal pronoun*, which should be used when you are the object of your own action, if you are talking about yourself and you are describing something you did or the way you feel about yourself, for example:

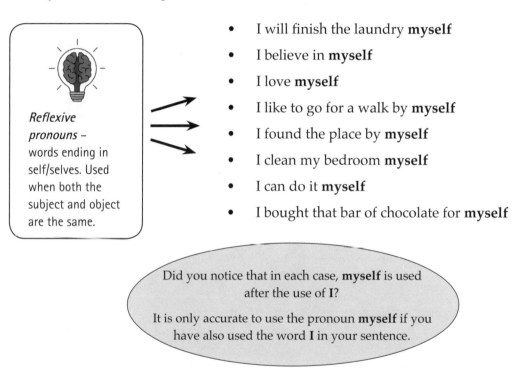

Reflexive pronouns – words ending in self/selves. Used when both the subject and object are the same.

- I will finish the laundry **myself**
- I believe in **myself**
- I love **myself**
- I like to go for a walk by **myself**
- I found the place by **myself**
- I clean my bedroom **myself**
- I can do it **myself**
- I bought that bar of chocolate for **myself**

Did you notice that in each case, **myself** is used after the use of **I**?

It is only accurate to use the pronoun **myself** if you have also used the word **I** in your sentence.

Have a look at the following statements, and circle whether you think they are correct or incorrect. The scoring key is at the end of the chapter.

1.	I do believe that I can do it by myself.	✓ ✗
2.	Emails can be sent to Clara or myself.	✓ ✗
3.	My friend called for my sister and myself.	✓ ✗
4.	I heard her singing that new song myself.	✓ ✗
5.	If you have any questions do not hesitate to contact me.	✓ ✗
6.	Please contact myself if you have any questions about this book.	✓ ✗

My physical and material self: Mine

We are turning once more to your English lessons on personal pronouns. **Me** and **mine** are both first person singular pronouns, however 'me' is just personal while 'mine' is personal *and* possessive.

Your physical self and appearance are important aspects of your personal identity. Your physical self refers to your body, the tangible aspect of you that can be directly observed, touched, examined and commented on. Therefore, your physical self-concept is your perception of yourself in terms of your physical appearance and ability. Your body or physical self is at the core of your material self.

> *Think about physical boundaries for a moment.*
>
> *Where do you end and another person begin?*

Our physical appearance and self-esteem are often closely related; we will return to the importance of self-esteem in Chapter 8. Our perception of how we look can have a big impact on the value we place on ourselves and how much confidence we have in our day-to-day lives. Physical appearance is an important aspect of personal identity and its relation to an individual's self-perception begins early in life.

Khloé Kardashian claimed in an interview that her mother said that she needed a nose job when she was just nine! We will revisit the pressures placed on physical appearance in Chapter 14 when we look at how the self navigates the social-media world of today.

Description of a 20-year-old woman's physical self:

I am average height and weight for a woman. I have an athletic build. I have long brown hair and green eyes. My ears are a bit big for the size of my face, but my hair covers them. I have great teeth and love to smile!

Describe your physical self.

_____

_____

_____

_____

You may have described your physical appearance, but did you include your brain? You may not have, probably because you can't physically see your brain day-to-day.

The self is distinct from the physical body. You may often say, 'I have a brain,' but it is unlikely that you might say things like, 'this body has a brain,' or 'this brain has a self.' You are more likely to say, 'I have a sense of self.'

Your material self also includes your possessions. For example your family possessions, your mobile phone, your car, your clothes, your friends, your body and your brain. We refer to these material possessions as **mine**.

Consider the following statements:

- That is a mobile phone

- That is my mobile phone

Once there is ownership attached to the phone, the meaning changes and it becomes more salient to you. This is the psychological impact of ownership.

Our possessions, just like our actions, are expressions of our selves.

Make a list of your five most valued possessions:

1.

2.

3.

4.

5.

What does your most prized possession say about you?

What do your material possessions say about you?

I identify with being in a musical family.

I am the sort of person who owns and drives a VW Caravelle (minibus) to keep my five children safe, and also to transport all their musical instruments, including a double bass and cello.

I identify with keeping my family safe, as opposed to driving a flashier car.

Did you get any other ideas about what type of person I am from the personal statements above?

Fill in the identity statement below based on your material self. This can be based on any possession that is of great importance to you and that you feel says something about who you are. Once you have completed your statement, develop two identity statements based on this articulation of your material self.

I am the sort of person who ...

How do you think others view you based on this material possession?

Selfies and shelfies

Selfies are a form of self-expression. As you know, they are pictures of oneself, taken by oneself, usually with a mobile phone and posted on social media, including networking sites such as Facebook and Snapchat. Selfies have become very popular – in 2013, the word 'selfie' was named 'word of the year' by the Oxford English Dictionary.

Shelfies are pictures of one's possessions which are also posted on social media and networking sites. The term shelfie was derived from the phenomenon of possessions artfully arranged on a shelf or some type of horizontal surface.

> *Do you post selfies or shelfies?*
>
> *What do you believe that they say about you?*

My husband often refers to shelfies as Lookatourstuff.com!

Chapter 14 will explore your self-presentations on social media.

Some more psychological concepts

Let us revisit the dual nature of self mentioned earlier. When you think of yourself as the doer *and* owner – as someone performing actions, and also as the owner of them – we can also use another term, known as *self-enactment*.

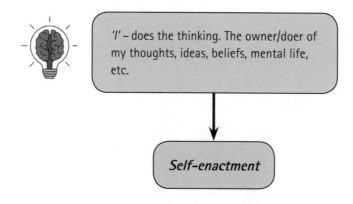

'I' – does the thinking. The owner/doer of my thoughts, ideas, beliefs, mental life, etc.

Self-enactment

When we are thinking thoughts about 'Me', these thoughts are how we make meaning and feel about ourselves, and therefore involve evaluations and judgements. Another term, *self-reflection*, describes the reflections and evaluations of your self-enactments, which again we will focus on in the next chapter.

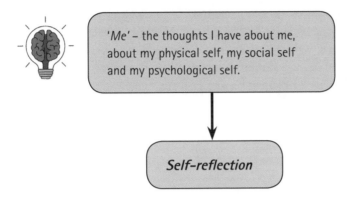

'*Me*' – the thoughts I have about me, about my physical self, my social self and my psychological self.

Self-reflection

My self and identity: My innermost core

I really believe that self and identity are the two most important terms used to talk about our wellbeing and how we describe ourselves. I believe that they represent the innermost core of who we are when we peel back the layers, and I feel privileged to be guiding and equipping you with the necessary tools to think about yourself in this meaningful way.

Self and identity are two closely related terms that I like to use together. We are talking about the dynamics of life, and therefore when we are meaning-making in the moment, we do not need to parse the terms any further. We will, however, make a distinction between the two terms for the purposes of understanding their development.

The self includes the term identity *within it*. Identity can be viewed like a tool we use to categorise and describe ourselves. When I carry out my own self-work, and have activated a particular memory and identity, I make sense of my own self and identity as combined at that moment.

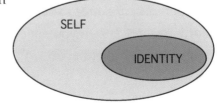

SELF

IDENTITY

The graphical representation below illustrates this point using identity categories which we will focus on in Chapter 5.

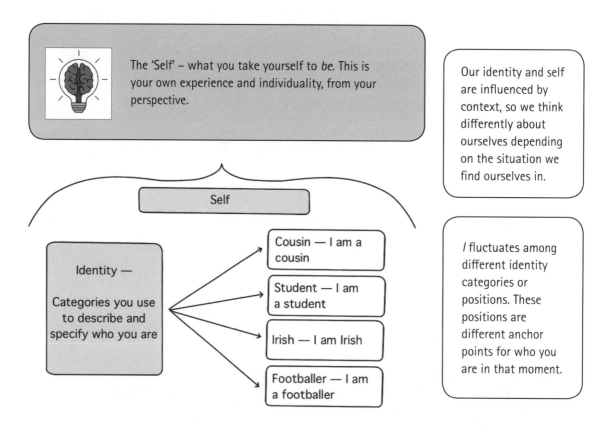

As well as identity categories, we also have identity markers. The most important to us is our name.

My name

Names are important in every culture of the world. It is by your name that you are first known and identified. Your name was most likely given to you by your parents on the day you were born, so you had no control over it; you had absolutely no say in the matter. When your parents announced your birth, one of the first things other people wanted to know was your name. So, before you are even aware of your name, people around you are using this identity marker about you.

During your first year of life, you began to grow into your name. You began to understand that the people around you called you this name and you began to react to it. Before you could even say your name, you already had an understanding of its importance in the social world around you, in your relationships with your parents and caregivers, with your siblings and your wider family.

> *Do you know when you first said your name?*
>
> *Do you remember introducing yourself on your first day of school?*

Questions about your name

Do you know why you were given your name? Maybe you were named after a famous musician or footballer, or was it a family tradition or name your parents loved?

You like or dislike your name because?

_____

_____

Is there a different name that you would have liked to have been called, and, if so, why?

_____

_____

Sometimes, we also have a nickname, which is another name that some people call us. This is sometimes a shortened version of your actual name that your friends use to refer to you, or maybe it is a pet name that your loved ones use. Maybe some people call you something different. For example, my dad was christened Myles Joseph Evans. As a child, I thought my dad's name was Joe, as Mam always called him that, and still does. My aunties and uncles call him Joey. I remember being so surprised when I heard his work colleagues call him Myles!

At the time, Dad explained to me that his dad was also named Myles, so he had been called Joey at home to avoid the confusion; he grew up being called Joe or Joey. So although his birth certificate clearly identifies my dad as Myles, he identifies more strongly as Joe.

Have you got a nickname?

_____

_____

Have a look at the example below, showing my own name and nicknames. I was christened Jennifer. In work and in formal situations, that is how I refer to myself: as Jennifer. I was Jenny at school and growing up. My friends call me Jen. I _prefer_ Jen. My parents called me Jennifer when I was in trouble. Jennifer in this context had a specific meaning.

I also had pet names at home. My parents called me Jen Wren or Jenny D (because my second name is Dolores, after my mam). Other than my husband and parents, no one else has ever called me these names. I also have another very special name – my children call me Mom, which is very important to me indeed.

My different names:

I also have an email address and a Facebook name.

Maybe you have a name for a Snapchat account too.

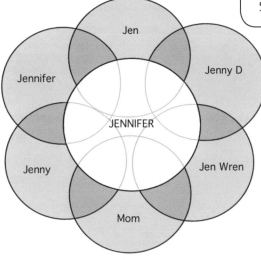

Now try one for yourself. With your formal name in the middle, fill in any other names that you are identified as.

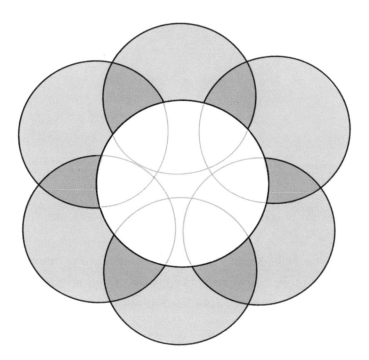

What does your name say about you?

_____

_____

_____

Maybe your name presents some identity information about you. For example, your nationality or family background.

My children all have Irish names. We identify very strongly with the Irish language, and the children all attend the gaelscoil (Irish primary school) and gaelcholáiste (Irish secondary school). My husband and I wanted to express our Irish identity in naming our children. They are named Clara, Maitiú, Oscar, Dáire and Rossa.

The cocktail party effect

This is a very interesting psychological phenomenon where a stimulus which is of significant value to you, such as hearing your name being spoken in someone's conversation, grabs your attention (even though you may not have been paying any attention to the conversation prior to hearing your name). This phenomenon demonstrates your ability to monitor your social environment for self-relevant cues in a non-conscious manner. This means that you did not set out to listen to see if anyone was going to say your name or was talking about you, but once you heard your name, it caught your attention.

This phenomenon occurs in my house all the time with my children. They stop in their tracks if they hear their names being used in my conversations, and will generally stop and try to listen to what is being said about them.

Take a moment and think of some occasions where this has happened to you.

Describe them below.

Constructing your first set of identity statements

In the first self-work activity in this chapter, you read through twelve statements and reflected on whether they applied to you or not. During this task, you were making decisions based on your current selfhood – on your own self and identity in that present moment. You may believe yourself to be a great athlete, and therefore you ticked the statement '*I am a great athlete*'. You may want to be an accountant when you are older because you love working with numbers, and therefore you did not tick the statement that you would love to be a teacher.

Now try another self-work activity. Make your own list of statements about yourself.

1. _____

2. _____

3. _____

4. _____

5. _____

6. _____

7. _____

8. _____

9. _____

10. _____

Once you have completed your list, have a look at the following question:

Did you refer to your personality traits, physical characteristics, your emotions, your relationships?

These statements are not only indicators of who you think you are, they are also indicators of what is of value to you. What parts of your identity appear to be the most salient?

Summary

What have you added to your psychological toolkit?

- You have considered the most fundamental question about being human, 'Who am I?', and have explored the answer, 'My self and identity.'

- You have explored some new psychological terms to help you understand and express your self and identity.

- You have created a description of your physical self.

- You have examined your material self in relation to your possessions, and compiled a list of your five most valued possessions. You also explored what these possessions say about you, as an expression of your identity.

- You briefly considered selfies and shelfies as forms of self-expression.

- You have investigated the importance of your name as an identity marker, and you developed a model of your different name identities.

- You have also explored the psychological phenomenon known as the cocktail party effect.

- Finally, you constructed your first set of identity statements.

Scoring key for activity – Myself or Me?

1. Correct

2. Incorrect

3. Incorrect

4. Correct

5. Correct

6. Incorrect

2 What Does Self-Work Involve?

Self is meaning-making!

We must make sense and meaning from our experiences, from all our thoughts, feelings and perceptions. Aldous Huxley very aptly noted that experience is not just what happens to us, but what we do with what happens to us,[1] while psychologists such as Jerome Bruner and Robert Kegan noted that the most universal thing about human experience is the phenomenon of self.[2–5] They refer to the ongoing experience of self and identity as it comes into being, develops and improves; we can think of our meaning-making context as ever changing and evolving, and always BECOMING – always moving. It is also useful to look at the words of the mathematician and philosopher Alfred Whitehead, who said that the most fundamental thing about life is that it *is* motion, rather than merely *in* motion.[6]

This is a very important message for you because it highlights the fact that you are never quite complete. Whenever you make a mistake or you do not perform as well as you had hoped on a task, don't be so hard on yourself! You are not finished: you still have plenty more to give and to improve on. This idea of becoming helps you to be more accepting and forgiving of yourself. You are an ongoing project; you can modify, improve and update.

Another well-known psychologist, Carl Rogers, based his theory of person-centred therapy around the concept of an *actualising tendency*, which he believed was the sole motive of personality. He described this tendency as an intrinsic push towards adaptation and growth in all living things; a motivation to fulfil our universal need to self-enhance and self-improve ourselves.[7]

In this chapter, you are going to:

- explore some new terminology from cognitive neuropsychology;

- think about yourself as ever-evolving, and never a finished project;

- apply some self-work activities to improve how you see yourself;

- consider the role played by your prefrontal lobes;

- evaluate the role played by your inner voice.

Carl Rogers was not the first to coin the term 'actualising tendency'; philosophers were already theorising about it in the early 1900s.

Self-work, metacognition and executive functioning skills

As noted in the previous chapter, *self-work* is an umbrella term that I use to describe the meaning-making processes we can use to make sense of, and understand, our self and identity.

The term *metacognition* refers to a regulatory system that people use to understand and control their own cognitive (brain) performance.

Executive functions are skills that we use to manage and regulate our everyday life. The field of cognitive neuropsychology produced the concept of executive functions, while metacognition arose from the field of developmental psychology. Both are now researched and utilised in many areas of psychology, including developmental, social, personality, clinical, forensic, cognitive, neuro- and biological psychology.

It can be useful to think of both executive functions and metacognition as supervising our thoughts about why we behave in certain ways, our emotional reactions to people and situations, our likes and dislikes, and our personality traits.

Metacognition is a self-regulatory process centred on managing your own thinking. In order to supervise and manage your own thinking, you can call on your executive functions.

Our executive functions are those self-regulatory actions that help us to plan and organise, focus and sustain our attention, and bring certain things into our working memory (for example, to keep goals and information in mind). They help us to refrain from responding immediately (to control our impulses), and to cope with and tolerate frustration. They also help us to consider the consequences of different behaviours, and how to plan out different scenarios. We call upon them in order both to reflect on our past experiences and to plan for our future.

> I like the metaphor of our executive functioning being like a conductor leading and directing the orchestra.

It is very clear that both these concepts are interrelated, and in fact the self-work activities that we carry out in developing and maintaining a positive self and identity involve integrating both these functions.

Metacognition is where we make our meaning. Our executive functions help support, and provide the scaffolding for, our metacognition. It therefore makes sense for us to group them together. This is apparent in the following examples.

Example 1: If you find yourself struggling to plan and organise (executive function skills) your study notes for an upcoming exam, just being aware of your struggle is thinking metacognitively.

Example 2: If you were struggling to make sense of why you overreacted in a certain situation, even though you had planned to stay calm (executive function skills), being aware of this struggle is the first step of metacognition.

Therefore, if you can **reflect** on **why** or **how** (meaning-making), then you can plan, evaluate and transform more efficiently, because you are thinking metacognitively.

In our second example, you can ask yourself: Why did I feel that way? Do I want to feel that way? Is that how I want to react? How could I avoid feeling that way in the future?

In later chapters, you will learn to self-question at a deeper level in relation to your social identity needs.

> We could refer to this as metacognitive questioning or self-regulatory questioning.

Below is an example of self-work skills combining metacognition and executive functioning:

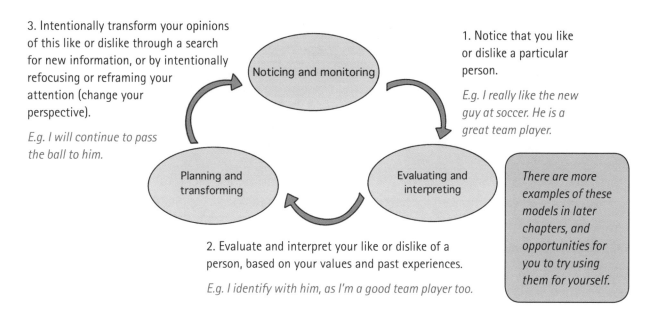

3. Intentionally transform your opinions of this like or dislike through a search for new information, or by intentionally refocusing or reframing your attention (change your perspective).

E.g. I will continue to pass the ball to him.

Noticing and monitoring

1. Notice that you like or dislike a particular person.

E.g. I really like the new guy at soccer. He is a great team player.

Planning and transforming

Evaluating and interpreting

There are more examples of these models in later chapters, and opportunities for you to try using them for yourself.

2. Evaluate and interpret your like or dislike of a person, based on your values and past experiences.

E.g. I identify with him, as I'm a good team player too.

The role of your brain: Prefrontal lobes and the prefrontal cortex

The neuropsychologist Elkhonon Goldberg first studied neuropsychology with its founding father, Alexander Luria, while at university in Russia. After relocating to the US, Goldberg made his own significant contribution to the field, investigating the importance of the prefrontal lobes. He found that this part of the brain is responsible for making us who we are, that it is where our sense of self and identity reside and, of course, where our inner voice resides.[8] He went on to publish an influential book on his findings, *The Executive Brain*.

René Descartes, the famous philosopher known for the phrase 'I think, therefore I am,' believed that the mind had a life of its own, independent of its own body.[9] You will not be at all surprised that this view is no longer accepted. Another great thinker, Antonio Damasio, coined the idea 'Descartes' error'![10]

Today, very few people would doubt that language, perception, cognition and memory reside within the brain. Even without any background in neurobiology, neuropsychology or neurology of any kind, one would not fall victim to the idea that the mind had a life of its own.

Later on in the workbook, you will also consider how 'the mind' involves our brain, our body and more! You will see how your cognitive processes also include your environment, including your social interactions, and physical objects (such as your phone, your computer and even your diary and journal exercises).

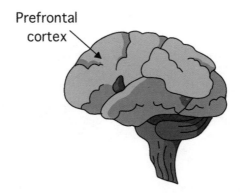

It has been established that the prefrontal lobes perform the most advanced and complex functions in your brain. In early studies, the focus of research was on the frontal lobes. For example, the neurologist Frederick Tilney termed human evolution at our time as the 'age of the frontal lobes'.[11]

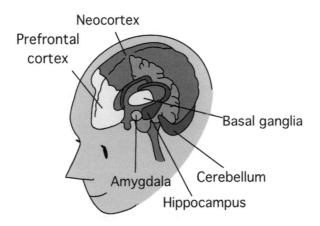

As you can imagine, as science advanced, and the technology produced more sophisticated instruments for investigating the brain, neurologists were able to pinpoint areas in the brain more accurately. For example, they could pinpoint the area which became known as the prefrontal lobe. This area is at the front of the frontal lobe, located above your eyebrows and beneath your forehead. The prefrontal lobes took centre stage, being considered 'the organ of civilization' in a famous work by Alexander Luria.[12,13]

With further scientific advancements, the prefrontal cortex (PFC) took over the spotlight. This is the very front of the prefrontal lobe, and is part of the wrinkled outer layer known as the cortex. The cortex refers to the dense outer layer of the brain that includes most of the brain's neurons. This outer layer is also known as the 'grey matter' of your brain. Therefore, it is not surprising that experimental studies suggest that the prefrontal cortex is the best-connected part of the brain – it is directly interconnected to every distinct unit of the brain.[14] It is this unique connectivity of the frontal and prefrontal lobes which makes them so suited for coordinating and integrating the work of the other brain structures.

We will see that human cognition can be forward looking and proactive, as opposed to merely reactive. In looking forward, we can set new goals and challenges. The emergence of the ability to formulate goals has been clearly linked to the emergence of the mental representations of self. It will therefore come as no surprise to you that the emergence of self-consciousness is also linked to the evolution of the prefrontal lobes.

> *It may surprise you that we are not always that effective in planning how we will feel in the future, and what our likes and dislikes will be. You will get to explore this difficulty later in this chapter when we look at affective forecasting.*

The development of the prefrontal lobes began to accelerate with the arrival of the Great Apes, which would eventually include Homo Sapiens, i.e. human beings.

The frontal lobes are the most uniquely human of all the components of the brain.

Many experiments have shown that the concept of 'SELF' appears only in the Great Apes, and it is only in the Great Apes that the prefrontal cortex acquires a major place in the brain.

Self-work activities and metacognition

We can practise and become more skilled at cognitive and metacognitive processes. The more you practise these skills, the better you will become at utilising them, as you will strengthen the neural pathways involved.

**METACOGNITION and EXECUTIVE FUNCTIONING
involved in SELF–WORK include:**

Self-regulation – involves understanding and managing your behaviour:

- being able to understand and manage strong emotional reactions like frustration, anger or embarrassment;

- being able to direct your attention to your social identity needs, and to certain behaviours to accomplish your goals.

Don't forget the example of metacognitive skills already presented earlier in this chapter.

We will focus on the role of social identity needs in directing our attention and behaviours in Chapter 5.

Self-questioning – you have been carrying out this self-work strategy since the beginning of this workbook.

Self-awareness and self-insight – you will explore this strategy shortly in this chapter.

Inner voice/self-talk – you will explore this strategy shortly in this chapter also.

> Are you motivated to understand and make sense of who you are?

Read through the following statements and, for each item, select one of the response choices, and write the number for your choice in the space provided.

Remember to answer as honestly and accurately as you can.

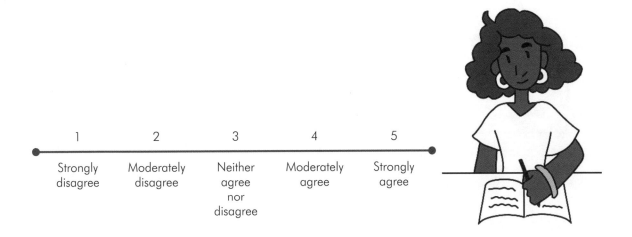

1	2	3	4	5
Strongly disagree	Moderately disagree	Neither agree nor disagree	Moderately agree	Strongly agree

1. I try to reflect on my thoughts and feelings as much as possible _____

2. I try to develop a realistic theory about why I behaved in a certain way _____

3. I am motivated to know why I feel the way I do _____

4. I am motivated to understand how my mind works _____

5. I am motivated to analyse and understand my behaviour _____

Total score _____

Interpreting your results

5	10	15	20	25

Low motivation
to understanding my
meaning-making

High motivation
to understanding my
meaning-making

Reflecting on your evaluation

Is your motivation to understand and make sense of who you are high, moderate or low?

Are you surprised at how you evaluated your motivation?

What have you learned about your motivation?

Self-awareness

Self-awareness simply refers to focusing on what is going on inside your head, inside your mind. By inside your mind, I mean an awareness and understanding of your emotions, your behavioural habits, your motives and desires, and of course your thoughts. Being self-aware involves closer communication with your self. Being aware of your cognitive processing, and being motivated to increase your knowledge of and trust in your own motives, desires, feelings and self-referent thoughts.

Examples of questions related to your self-awareness:

- How motivated are you to do well in your mathematics exam?

- Do you intend to go to college or not?

- Are you planning to be famous?

Below, write down some examples of you being self-aware.

-

-

-

-

-

There are numerous self-work strategies you can use to help you become more self-aware:

- Take the time to name your thoughts and emotions. Ask questions like:

  ◊   Why do I feel this way?

  ◊   Do I want to feel like this?

  ◊   What made me draw that conclusion?

  ◊   Do I want to react this way?

- Keep a journal or make journal entries in a workbook like this one.

- Set goals and monitor whether you are achieving them.

- Be honest with yourself; it's so simple, but so important.

- Keep in mind the cognitive biases that you will explore shortly in this chapter.

- Can you think of anything else that you could do to become more self-aware?

- Remember that you are a work in progress, so try not to be too critical of yourself and who you are.

Awareness of the here and now is obviously very important, but there is also an important role played by your memory and the self-knowledge that you have organised and stored within it, which we will explore in the next chapter.

Your inner voice

'Of course I talk to myself; sometimes I need expert advice on who I am or why I reacted in a certain way.'

We express a story to others, but also to ourselves, of who we are. This unique inner voice is your silent expression of conscious thought to yourself. Your inner voice, this verbal thinking or self-talk, is important for self-work because silently verbalising is an important organising tool for planning and sense-making.

In order to build healthy concepts of ourselves, and to remain in a positive state of mind, it is important to continue to develop and to stay closely aware of who we truly are. We are all wonderfully different and unique, and we can all think positively about ourselves through our inner voice.

Take a moment. Be mindful of your inner voice.

Think of how much time during the day consists of inner speech; it is very significant. We do it when we are planning, problem-solving, self-monitoring, reading, writing, calculating and thinking back on events.

Our inner voice interacts with:

- working memory to enhance coding of new material;
- rehearsing past interactions, situations, emotions;
- past recall of personal events – autobiographical memory;
- future scenario planning and creativity;
- self-regulation and self-awareness.

The next chapter deals with these aspects of your memory.

Who is this little voice inside my head asking all these questions?

_____

I expect that you wrote your name down as the person talking. In my case it is Jennifer that is talking. Jennifer is the identifier.

It is (add your name) _____ that is talking, during common, everyday experiences.

It is (add your name) _____ that is the last person I listen to before I fall asleep, and the first person to talk when I wake up.

Noam Chomsky, a really influential linguist, presented a lecture at Carleton University called 'Language and the Cognitive Science Revolution(s)' in 2011. You can watch it on YouTube.[15]

In this lecture, Chomsky notes that 'if you introspect, you can't go one minute without talking to yourself. It takes a tremendous act of will not to talk to yourself.'

Why not take the challenge and see how long you can actually last before some word or thought comes into your mind. It won't be long at all.

You can try this on a friend. See how long they can last before they talk to themselves. This is universal; it takes huge effort to keep from talking to oneself in every waking moment.

There are numerous linguists who propose that the purpose of language is for communication. I believe that language is a very important communicative tool, however, there is another important function of language, and that is its role in how we structure our thoughts. Noam Chomsky presented the role of language as a system for expressing thought, and this had a huge impact on psychology, and, in particular, on psycholinguistics.

In the Welcome chapter, I mentioned that you would soon become a fluent user of the psychological language of self and identity. For example in Chapter 1, we looked at the psychological concepts of 'I' and 'Me', and 'Me' versus 'Myself'. These psychological concepts add structure to your thoughts in a certain way that will enable you to make sense and meaning of yourself.

This reminds me of a term put forward by William James a very long time ago, which I think is fantastic here: **'Psychologising'**.[16] As you become fluent in your use of the psychological terminology of self and identity, you are indeed psychologising. Psychologising to a more positive self and identity, and sense of wellbeing.

Cognitive behavioural therapy and our inner voice

Aaron Beck is known as the father of cognitive behavioural therapy (CBT). His focus was on how our emotions and behaviours are caused by our internal dialogue; our inner voice. He proposed that we can change ourselves by learning to challenge and question our own thoughts, in particular, by focusing on specific cognitive biases and problematic thought patterns such as being too hard on ourselves when we make a mistake.[17]

Non-verbal signals of communication

Remember that other people around you only know what your inner voice is saying by what you overtly tell them. In philosophy, this is referred to as the problem of other minds. However, there are other ways of communicating with others such as through body language. Body language refers to the non-verbal signals that we can use to communicate. The most obvious of these are our facial expressions.

Have a look at the following emotions and write down what type of facial expressions would communicate the corresponding emotion. I've completed the first one for you.

Happiness	Smile (you can smile with your mouth and your eyes)
Confusion	_____
Sadness	_____
Surprise	_____
Anger	_____
Disappointment	_____
Excitement	_____
Fear	_____

Think of how prevalent the use of emojis have become as expressions of how we feel. I must say I rely quite a lot on them myself when I'm texting friends and I want a quick way to express the emotional tone of the message.

The expression on your face can also help other people decide if they believe what you are saying. A hand over a mouth while talking, pursed lips, and not making direct eye contact are often cited as signs someone is not telling the truth.

Bodily gestures are also expressions of a person's intentions. For example, a clenched fist might indicate that a person is very angry. A thumbs up may indicate that someone agrees with you, or that all is going to plan, whereas a thumbs down expresses something very different: that someone is not happy with the situation. Crossed arms and hands on hips can also express discontent or anger.

Can you think of any more non-verbal signals?

Being aware of our cognitive biases

Within cognitive psychology, numerous cognitive biases have been investigated. These are mistakes that we make in our judgements; in our thinking and reasoning. This is a huge area of research which documents a large number of the cognitive biases we are susceptible to. Here we will focus on some of the biases which can affect how we make sense of ourselves and our self-work.

Self-serving bias – this is a tendency to blame external forces when things go wrong, and give yourself the full credit when things go well. This can occur quite a lot when you consider that we are motivated to enhance and maintain our self-esteem.

Optimism bias – this is a tendency to believe that you are more likely to be successful and less likely to fail compared to others.

Confirmation bias – this is a tendency to favour information that conforms to your existing beliefs about yourself and to disregard evidence that does not fit into your existing beliefs. This often occurs when you read your horoscope.

The Dunning–Kruger effect – this is a tendency to believe that you are smarter and more able than you really are.

Making future predictions

Affective forecasting is a self-work activity involving making predictions about how you will feel in the future. This type of activity involves predicting our future emotions, whether they will be positive or negative, whether they will be very intense, and whether they will have a long or short duration. Dan Gilbert and Tim Wilson have found that we can be quite ineffective at predicting our emotions[18] – their research has revealed that we are not always as happy as we thought we would be when we get the things we want.

Think of a time when you were really excited about something, but when it happened it didn't please you or satisfy you to the extent that you had initially anticipated. Describe this incident.

Have a look at the numerous TED Talk videos by Dan Gilbert on the surprising science of happiness and the psychology of the future self.[19] What kind of strategies could you use to improve your affective forecasting?

Summary

What have you added to your psychological toolkit?

- You have considered how your human experience is a work in progress, which is ever changing and always becoming.

- You have learned about and explored some examples of metacognitive and executive functioning skills, including the model illustrating the process of noticing and monitoring, evaluating and interpreting, and planning and transforming.

- You have learned about the role played by the prefrontal lobes, and the emergence of self-consciousness in the brain.

- You have assessed your motivation to understand and make sense of who you are.

- You have answered questions related to your self-awareness, and developed some examples of your self-awareness.

- You even suggested some strategies to help you become more self-aware.

- You explored being mindful of how much you rely on your inner voice, and how much time every day consists of your inner speech.

- You challenged yourself to see how long you could last before a word came into your head.

- You considered what types of facial expressions communicate different emotions.

- You also described a situation where you over-emphasised how happy you would be in the future.

- You watched some TED Talk videos by Dan Gilbert, explaining the mistakes we make when we are planning how we will feel in the future.

3 The Remembering Self: My Self-Knowledge Memory Store

Our continuous sense of self is preserved in our memory

When you think about or report on your identity, you are reflecting upon and describing your own behaviours either currently in the present moment or in the past. For example, if a person describes themselves as shy, they may be thinking back to situations where they had very little to say in front of others, or maybe they avoided public speaking, or found it hard to make friends.

You are now very much aware that it is important to devote time to managing ourselves when carrying out self-work. We need to spend time thinking about how we make sense and meaning of our experiences. Remembering and looking back on our actions, feelings and emotions is a primary source of meaning-making for us.

We will see in this chapter that our *working memory* and *autobiographical memory* give us the capacity to use information from the past in the present, and also to help make predictions about the future.

In this chapter, you are going to:

- develop an appreciation of the role played by memory in understanding and knowing yourself;

- learn about the different theories of memory, and the central executive system.

Self as a knower

We have already considered how useful our inner voice is to view the self as the meaning-making activity of being a person. This meaning-making activity of self includes the interplay of our beliefs, thoughts, emotions and our social interactions.

We did some work on the dual function of the self in Chapter 1. Remember that the self can also be the object; an idea or mental representation of the self. **I** is the thinker, and also who the thoughts are about.

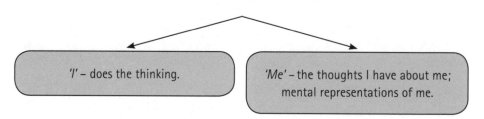

'I' – does the thinking.

'Me' – the thoughts I have about me; mental representations of me.

Your mental representations of your self and identity involve self-knowledge, what you know about your beliefs, thoughts, memories, feelings and values. These are your own, and are unique to you, and they are different from those of your friends, family and significant others.

Unique self-knowledge mental representations

Beliefs

Thoughts

Memories

Feelings

Values

Personality traits

Competencies, skills, abilities, knowledge

As you might already have guessed, you have thousands of mental representations! Obviously, you can't bring all your mental representations into your attention at once, so where is all your self-knowledge stored? What happens is that you pull from events from the past as you make sense of things – your memory of the past provides a record of your lifetime of experienced events, and of the knowledge that you have acquired along the way. Your memory can also affect your experience of what is happening to you right now in this given moment. At any given time, activated self-knowledge comes to the fore, or becomes salient (important), while the remaining self-knowledge remains unattended.

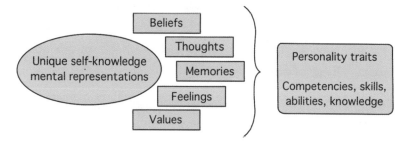

Memory is the mental system for keeping, storing, retrieving and using information about stimuli, images, events, ideas and skills, after the original information is no longer present. It stores our knowledge, experiences and skills over time so that they are available to us when later required.

Memory is life

I particularly like how Tennessee Williams describes memory and the present moment in his play *The Milk Train Doesn't Stop Here Anymore* as being 'all memory except for the one present moment that goes by you so quickly that you hardly catch it going'.[1]

Michael Gazzaniga, a prominent psychologist in charge of the SAGE Center for the Study of the Mind at the University of California, also refers to memory alongside the present moment, stating that 'everything in life is memory, save for the thin edge of the present'.[2] These descriptions give a very strong image of how much of the mind involves memory.

The thin edge of the present is where your sense of self resides. This is your personal identity (which we will discuss further in the next chapter). It refers to what is happening right now but, a moment from now, the present will become the past and you may or may not store it as a memory.

'Tennessee' is the better-known nickname of Thomas Lanier Williams III, an American playwright of the twentieth century. Here you see that he created a public identity around his nickname. Recall in Chapter 1, we looked at names and nicknames as identity indicators.

I love the metaphor of memory as a time machine. You can go back to just a few moments ago, to the words that you read at the beginning of this sentence, or to many years ago, to events as far back as your first day at school. This mental time travel plays a key role in our self and identity and self-knowledge.

What are the functions of our memory system?

Take a moment to think of the important functions of your memory. Make a list of the five most important things you use your memory for.

1.

2.

3.

4.

5.

In making this list, it may help you to think about how important your memory is in your day-to-day life. You may have mentioned things like remembering material in exams, keeping track of your daily schedule, names of people, directions to places, and so on. But did you consider more basic functions?

Consider the use of memory in an everyday example, such as knowing how to get the bus.

You need to know the sequence of events, starting with checking the bus timetable ahead of time, waiting at the correct bus stop, getting on the bus when it stops, paying the correct fare, sitting down in a free seat, watching out for your stop to get off at the end of the journey, ringing the bell when it is time to get off, among countless other small but important details.

You also may not have considered how important your memory is to keep track of the flow of a conversation with your friend or with those around you.

Memory research and real life

In traditional memory studies, participants were asked to memorise information given to them and then recall it. The participants memorised information only because the investigator had given them instructions to do so. In most real life situations, we store and recall information not for the sake of recall itself, but as a necessary precursor for solving day-to-day problems. In our example of taking the bus, we are not being told what to recall, we ourselves decide what stored information is useful.

Stages of memory

Encoding

Information from the environment is constantly reaching your senses in the form of *stimuli*. Encoding allows you to change the stimuli so that you can put it into your memory.

This is also referring to *experience*, and how you organise and make sense of what happens to you.

Stimulus – an event or object which triggers a response. For example, hearing your name being called, or witnessing a car crash.

Storage

Once you have experienced and encoded information, you will then store it in your brain. You may encode it in a way that makes it last a lifetime in your long-term memory, or lasts a much shorter time in your short-term memory.

Retrieval

The memories that you have stored will, at times, need to be recalled. Whether you can remember something or not depends on the way that it was stored, and the cues that were used to access the information. Information that was stored in a meaningful way is easier to retrieve.

We will look at an example of this in the self-reference effect.

The self-reference effect

The self-reference effect is a really interesting memory recall tendency related to self, suggesting that we recall more information when we try to relate it to ourselves.

In the psychology labs that I ran many years ago, we would carry out a computerised self-reference experiment. The hypothesis was that participants would have more accurate recall for words processed in terms of themselves compared to words processed according to more superficial qualities.

Participants were presented with words and asked if the word had any relevance to them in relation to their personality or if the word contained the letter 'E' in it (this was the superficial quality). At the recall, participants remembered more of the words which were related to themselves; we generally found support for the self-reference effect and for our hypothesis.

There have been numerous metaphorical models and theories of memory put forward in cognitive psychology. We will first look at the *multi-store model of human memory* which has served a very important historical function, as it was the first systematic account of the structures of our memory. The conceptual distinction between three different types of memory – *sensory*, *short-term* and *long-term* memory – still makes sense today.

Multi-store model of memory (Richard Atkinson and Richard Shiffrin)[3]

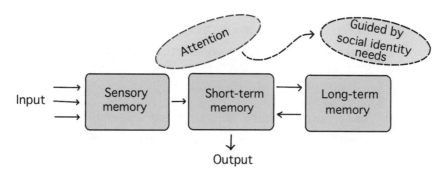

This explanation of memory assumes that there are three separate memory stores: sensory, short-term, and long-term; and that information is transferred between these stores in a linear fashion. Each memory store differs in the way information is processed (encoding), how much information can be stored (capacity), and for how long (duration). It has been described as an information processing model (like a computer) with an input, process and output.

Information that has gained your attention enters sensory memory. Information is stored as a fleeting impression of sensory stimuli. If this is attended to, this information enters the short-term memory, and if the information is given meaning (elaborative rehearsal), it is passed on to the long-term memory.

> You will see in Chapter 4 that your attention can be guided by your social identity needs.

Cognitive psychology has carried out numerous studies investigating this model. At a very general level, the model can be criticised for focusing on the structural aspects of memory at the expense of an adequate view of the processes involved in learning and memory. The spatial metaphor of memory, as 'boxes in the mind', can also prevent us from seeing memory as an active process.

Depths of processing approach to memory (Fergus Craik and Robert Lockhart)[4]

Fergus Craik and Robert Lockhart proposed the *levels of processing model* as a reaction to the boxes-in-the-mind model. The very simple idea behind this model is that the level or depth at which we process information determines how well it is remembered (we have already touched on this idea above with the self-reference effect).

At shallow levels, you might analyse physical or sensory stimuli such as the brightness of light, or the pitch of musical notes. The by-product of these analyses are memory traces. Such stimuli may be quickly forgotten, as the memory trace will be fragile due to the brief cognitive processing involved. The deep levels involve analysis in terms of meaning. For example, when you analyse for meaning, you may think of other related images or past experiences. These types of memory traces will be more resilient due to the extra cognitive processing, the extra time spent thinking about and making meaning, and hence they are more likely to be remembered.

Working memory (Alan Baddeley and Graham Hitch)[5]

The *working memory* is the part of the short-term memory that allows your brain to hold on to information for a brief period of time so that you can carry out cognitive tasks. In *The Emotional Brain*, Joseph LeDoux puts forward an idea which has been adopted by many contemporary cognitive scientists: that consciousness is the awareness of what is in working memory.[6]

Working memory is a limited capacity system, where information is held for a brief period so that you can carry out cognitive tasks such as reading, comprehension and assessing needs.

What cognitive research has taught us about working memory – it:

- receives information from multiple stores;

- holds information for a few seconds (it is temporary);

- can hold only five to seven items at a time (it has small capacity);

- holds and manipulates information, a cognitive workspace;

- depends on control of attention and mental effort.

In the 1970s, cognitive psychologists Alan Baddeley and Graham Hitch extended the definition of working memory, which resulted in the idea of a *central executive system*. This is where we will turn our attention next.

The central executive system (CES) and working memory

This is actually an attention controller, not a memory system!

Phonological loop

Verbal and auditory information.

E.g. trying to remember a person's name, or when you read a book.

Central executive

(cognitive control network)

The majority of working memory occurs here. You pull information from your long-term memory, and coordinate the activity of both the phonological loop and visuospatial sketch pad by focusing on specific parts of a task and switching attention from one part to another. An important task in itself is deciding how to divide attention between different tasks.

Visuospatial sketch pad

Visual and spatial information.

E.g. when you are forming an image of what your friend looks like in your mind, or doing a jigsaw.

The episodic or sensory buffer is temporary storage that binds both auditory and visuospatial information in the present moment, and can draw on information from long-term memory.

Remember your inner voice inside your head. This silent rehearsal plays a central role here in short-term memory, in the phonological loop (we will look at this again shortly).

Incoming information from your senses needs to be temporarily stored (for a few 100s of milliseconds) in order to be able to compete for your attention.

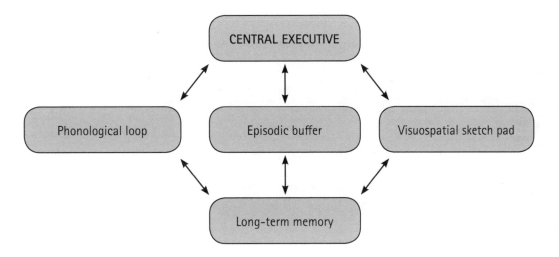

The central executive system is a psychological system that functions to control cognitive processes. What this really means is that you are in control; you are the conductor. Throughout this workbook, you are learning to be an effective positive conductor of your own thoughts and actions.

The central executive system organises processing and storage resources for carrying out cognitive processes. It flexibly allocates central processing and storage for completion of goals, for example the fulfilment of social identity needs, which we will explore in the next chapter.

For now though, we will just note that when a social identity need is activated – for example your need to do well in an exam, for a sense of achievement, self-efficacy, pride and status – this directs the focus of your central executive system. This is where your goals, and your cognitive and storage resources, are implemented until completion of the exam. Your working memory holds these cognitive states active to attain your goal.

Alan Baddeley – YouTube videos worth watching:

- 'The origins of the central executive'
- 'On the development of the working memory model'
- 'Introduction of the phonological loop'
- 'Introduction of the episodic buffer'[7]

 Do you remember in the last chapter when we thought about our inner voice? You can probably imagine that your inner voice is very important as a means of silent rehearsal. Silent rehearsal occurs in your temporary working memory (phonological loop). Silently verbalising is so important in thinking and awareness, and it also helps in planning, problem-solving, reading, writing and, more importantly here, for self-motivating and for your autobiographical memory. Your inner speech has a positive influence on many cognitive tasks.

Just think about how much you talk to yourself when you are planning to carry out a task, even if it is simply picking all the clothes off your bedroom floor and sorting them for the laundry!

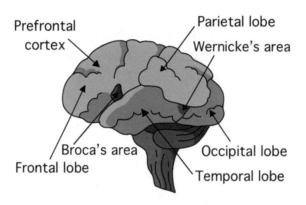

Strategies to improve your working memory (your mental clipboard)

You are likely familiar with the importance of your physical fitness, for your wellbeing. You may not be as familiar with the concepts of mental and brain fitness, which refer to keeping your emotional health and your brain in good shape. This has become a very important area of investigation for improving our wellbeing and our brain performance.

Many neuropsychologists in this field (for example, Richard Haier at the Mind Research Network and the research team led by Susanne Jaeggi) are interested in the effects of regular brain exercise on our cognitive functioning and our brain power. Remember in Chapter 2 we looked at the prefrontal cortex area of the brain, which contains most of the brain's neurons. It is further proposed that regular brain exercise increases the thickness of the brain's cortex and can actually create new neurons.

With our smartphones always handy, it is easy to forget how much information you keep in your head day-to-day. There are numerous things you can do to improve your working memory, for example:

- practise holding a person's address in mind while listening to instructions about how to get there;

- try listening to a sequence of events in a story while trying to understand what the story means;

- learn a new instrument and learn to sight read;

- learn a new language.

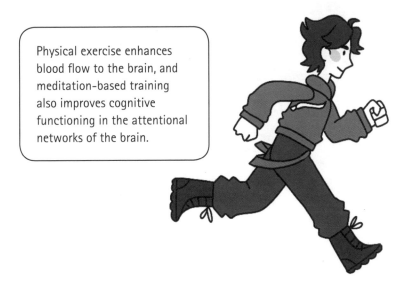

Richard Haier believes that because our brains are remarkably adaptive we can train and improve our cognitive abilities using computer games. He found significant evidence that the video game *Tetris* improves our cognitive functioning.

You can access an interview with Haier on YouTube ('Proof that *Tetris* makes you smarter'[8]), where he gives a detailed account of how playing *Tetris* improves cognitive functioning.

Physical exercise enhances blood flow to the brain, and meditation-based training also improves cognitive functioning in the attentional networks of the brain.

Due to inconsistent scientific results, there has been a lot of debate on the effectiveness of brain-training. In an effort to resolve this debate, Susanne Jaeggi, Anja Pahor and Aaron Seitz have undertaken a programme of research investigating whether brain-training actually works. They believe that the lack of consensus is due to the wrong scientific questions being investigated.[9]

Remember in the Welcome chapter that we considered the importance of the research question.

You can access https://socialsciences.nature.com/posts/who-benefits-from-brain-training to take a look for yourself. A lot of research has focused on the effects of brain-training on the general public, working with averages and with a one-size-fits-all approach. Just like diet and physical exercise, brain-training does not benefit everyone in the exact same way. Therefore, questions formulated around specific groups of people, or indeed at a more individual level, are needed in order to produce more meaningful and useful data.

Long-term memory

Your long-term memory is like an archive of information about past events that you have experienced in your life, and knowledge about people, things and events that you have learned along the way.

We have already mentioned that this storage stretches from just a few minutes ago to as far back as you can actually remember. We have access to this resource as we go about our daily lives. In the play *The Importance of Being Earnest*, Oscar Wilde describes memory as 'the diary that we all carry about with us'.[10]

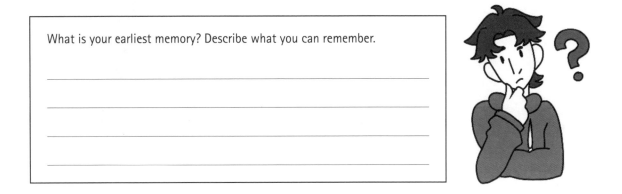

What is your earliest memory? Describe what you can remember.

There are different types of memories investigated in cognitive psychology and neuropsychology that are really interesting.

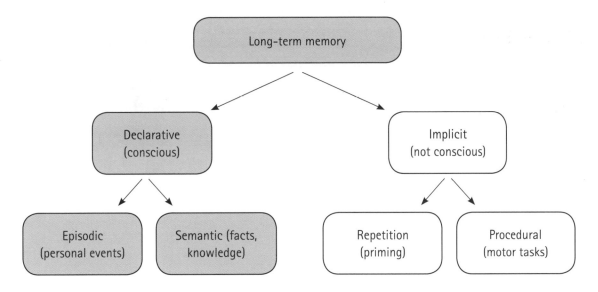

Here we will just look at declarative (conscious) knowledge, as our focus in this book is on intended and deliberate meaning-making.

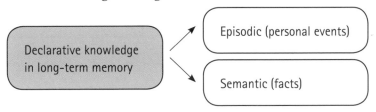

You have probably already guessed that this type of episodic memory is where we can mentally time travel. This type of self-knowing and remembering allows you to put yourself back in a situation through mental time travel. It is very important to keep in mind that this does not guarantee that the memory is accurate. Memories of events from our past do not always correspond to what actually happened.

The constructive nature of memory is really interesting; what you report as memories are constructed by you based on what actually happened plus additional factors such as your knowledge, experiences and expectations. Memory can be modified or created by suggestion, and your mood at the time of recall or at the time of the actual event can have an impact on what is remembered!

Can you recall a time when both yourself and a friend, parent or family member remembered an event differently?

_____

_____

_____

_____

_____

_____

_____

_____

_____

_____

_____

_____

In the Welcome chapter, you considered journalling as a written record of who you are; of yourself and your identity. *Autobiographical memory* allows you to recall personal experiences that are important in your life. When you remember the events that make up the stories of your life, when you place yourself back in a specific situation, you are experiencing your autobiographical/episodic memory, using your ability to mentally time travel.

What determines the life events that you will remember years later?

Make a list of some personal milestones which you feel have impacted on how you view yourself.

_____

_____

_____

_____

_____

_____

Examples of some significant milestones include:

- graduating from school or college;

- receiving your school or college results;

- winning a prestigious award or competition;

- highly emotive events such as an illness or accident, e.g. COVID-19;

- the death of a loved one.

Did you change your view of yourself based on any of these milestones?

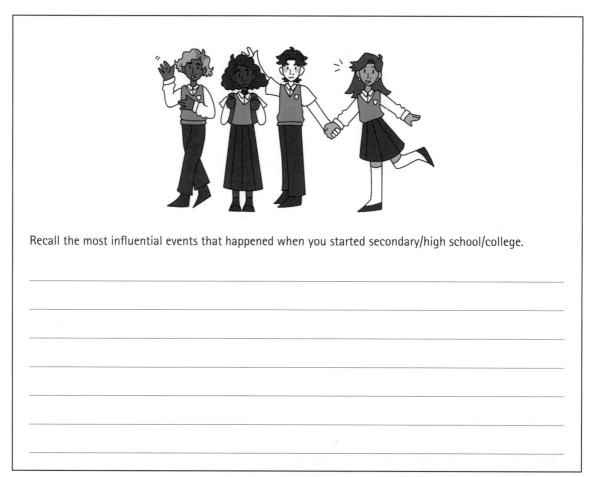

Recall the most influential events that happened when you started secondary/high school/college.

_____

_____

_____

_____

_____

_____

_____

Did most of the events you recalled occur during September? You often remember things more clearly at the beginning of a new situation as the experience is novel, and then you begin to get used to it.

It should be becoming apparent to you that you form your identity by integrating your life experiences into an internalised evolving story of who you are, and that this provides you with a sense of unity and purpose in your life. It is generally assumed that adolescence and young adulthood are a very special time for encoding memories of who you are.

Make a list of some of the most significant firsts that you can remember in your life so far.

First day of college
First disco
First partner
First job

Summary

What have you added to your psychological toolkit?

- You have considered yourself as a knower of your likes, feelings, values and memories.

- You have explored the functions and stages of your memory.

- You have explored the self-reference effect.

- You have learned about the different theories of memory, and the importance of working memory for your sense of self and self-work activities.

- You have considered the importance of your long-term memory for knowing who you are.

- You challenged yourself to recall significant memories that have played an important role in understanding who you are.

4 My Motivating Social Identity Needs

We are all wanters and knowers. You explored yourself as a knower in the previous chapter. In this chapter, you are turning your attention to considering yourself as a wanter; you are thinking of all the wants and desires that you experience. These wants can be achievements, friendships, material things, etc.

As a wanter, *motivation* is used to describe why you choose some activities over others, and why you persist at certain activities. Throughout this workbook, I am proposing that the self and identity are very important motivational terms. They are very important for understanding what motivates you. How you view the world, your likes and dislikes, why you sometimes worry.

We have a fundamental need to maintain and enhance our sense of self. We are also motivated to behave in ways that are consistent with our existing positive self-views of ourselves; our established self-perceptions.

In this chapter, you are going to:

- consider yourself as a wanter, and learn about motivation;

- learn about your fundamental social identity needs;

- explore three types of social identity needs, which guide you toward the construction and maintenance of your positive sense of who you are, in your past, present and future.

Motivation: Self as a wanter

As a system, our self and identity is dynamic and motivated. We are motivated to enhance and protect our self-esteem, and our positive self and identity. We will first consider motivation in general and then progress to *social identity needs*, which are the guiding forces toward the creation and maintenance of a positive self and identity.

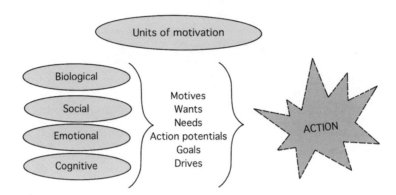

Broadly, the term motivation refers to biological, emotional, social and cognitive forces that activate behaviour. These forces causing you to act have been defined using words like motives, needs, desires, wants, drives, goals and action potentials. I like to use the terms needs and goals, as we use these terms very comfortably every day. We use the term motivation to describe why we did something, as the driving force behind our actions. We are also interested in the factors that direct and maintain our actions, why we choose certain behaviours over others, and why we persist at certain tasks.

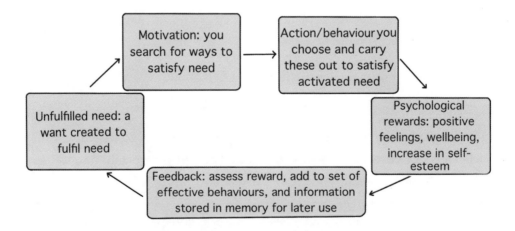

We will define a *need* as a concept that stands for a force or a drive which organises our perception, our thoughts and actions to fulfil the unsatisfied need. In other words, we are moved or motivated to fulfil an activated need – therefore satisfying the need becomes the goal of our activity.

I began investigating the field of motivation in the mid-'90s. I was intrigued by the body of knowledge which benefitted from so many areas in psychology, from cognitive, neuropsychology, developmental and social to educational. In our quest to feel positive about ourselves, it is generally accepted that we experience the following universal needs. Read through the list below, and tick if you believe the statement applies to you – don't be surprised if you tick them all!

We are motivated to fulfil the need for friendships, social contact and the need to belong.	
We are motivated to fulfil the need to be in control of our decision-making, and to feel a sense of control in our lives.	
We are motivated to master activities and tasks that are of value to us, and to develop a sense of accomplishment.	
We are motivated to seek balance in our thoughts, and in our self-views.	
We are motivated to fulfil a need to feel unique and distinct from others.	
We are motivated to reduce feelings of uncertainty, and to create a sense of meaning in our lives.	
We are motivated to create a sense of connection or continuity to our past and our future.	
We are motivated to enhance our view of ourselves, to increase our self-esteem and social status.	

I hope that it is becoming clearer to you that the self and identity are very important motivational constructs, because our goals, needs and motives are dependent on how we view ourselves. We are also motivated to behave in ways that are consistent with our existing positive self-views of ourselves, our established self-perceptions. Ultimately, we all have a need for a positive sense of self and identity, so it is important to understand how we can fulfil this need.

Our needs for a positive self and identity

In this section, we will look at three types of needs: *affiliation*, *autonomy* and *esteem*. We will refer to them as social identity needs, as we are motivated to fulfil them in order to satisfy our need for a positive sense of self and self-worth. They are therefore essential for our well-being and our psychological growth.

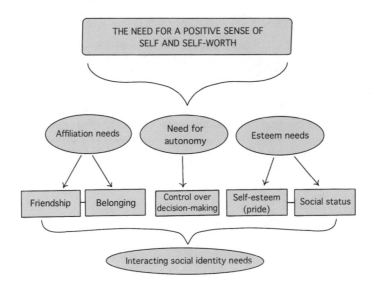

Social identity needs of affiliation

No one could deny that we are motivated towards social contact. The need for affiliation refers to our need to be in close contact with others, and to cooperate or reciprocate with an allied other or friend. I believe, like many others, that there are two closely related elements that are involved in the need for affiliation: the need for friendship and the need to belong.

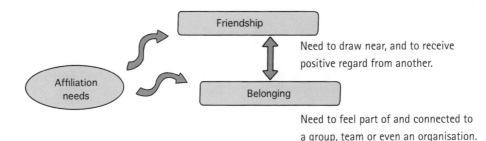

We won't carry out any self-work activities here on our social identity needs, as there are full chapters focusing on each type of need in Part 2 of the workbook. In Chapter 6, you will have the opportunity to explore your needs for friendship and belonging.

Social identity need for autonomy

The second social identity need considered important for the development and maintenance of your positive self and identity, and personal worth, is the need for autonomy. The importance of the need for autonomy or competence for self-worth has long been recognised – we are motivated to be in control of our decision-making, and to be independent.

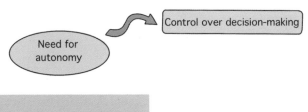

In Chapter 7, you will have the opportunity to explore your need for autonomy in detail.

Social identity needs for esteem (pride) and social status

You are probably quite clear at this point that you have a fundamental drive to maintain or enhance your phenomenal self, and of course your self-esteem. As far back as the late 1800s, William James was already describing self-esteem as an elementary endowment of human nature.[1] Self-esteem is a focal need in your social identity processes.

Think about this for a moment.

Could you ever really accept that you were inherently no good, that you were useless?

The full conscious belief in such an idea is something I believe we try to avoid at all costs, and so we strive to enhance and maintain a positive view of ourselves.

Abraham Maslow was a very well-known motivation thinker – you may have come across his *hierarchy of needs* theory.[2] Here, we are interested in how he conceptualised self-esteem as the need for self-respect and for reputation. That we have a need or desire for a stable and high evaluation of ourselves, and also respect from others.

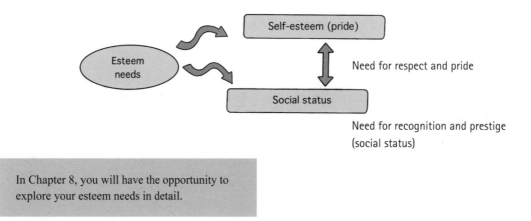

In Chapter 8, you will have the opportunity to explore your esteem needs in detail.

The social identity needs of affiliation, autonomy and esteem interact in dynamic ways. This interaction is evident in the following example:

Ms Murphy decided to give her students the opportunity to express their opinions and ideas on how their classroom should be arranged and how their tables should be set up. This resulted in the students feeling more connected and satisfied in their role as class members. They identified more with their class and teacher when they were granted respect and status and felt more control over their class environment.

In exploring this interaction, we can get a fuller picture and understanding of what is going on when we are motivated to develop and maintain a positive self and identity.

Your social identity needs guide your past knowledge

You have already explored in the previous chapter on the remembering self that stored self-knowledge (memories) in your short- and long-term memory (autobiographical) consists of self-knowledge relating to past experiences and observations of your own behaviours.

This stored self-knowledge is held in memory and is not always being attended to. The majority of it is awaiting a time to be reactivated by you. I agree with the work of Jacky Swan and colleagues,[3] that although stored self-knowledge is at least theoretically accessible to conscious awareness, only information in the working memory (as discussed in the previous chapter), is available for immediate reflection.

Social identity needs guiding stored self-knowledge and the past self: Who you remember yourself as

An example of social identity needs influencing the retrieval of past stored information:

Your activated social identity needs, such as the need to do well in your music exam, can direct your past memories – maybe you got a really high mark in your last exam?

This memory becomes activated and reminds you of how good it felt to do so well, and further motivates you to keep working towards your goal: the present self communicates to your future self about your past self.

Try for yourself. Describe a time when your present self coordinated with your past and future selves.

Your social identity needs guide your active self-knowledge

As you now know, active self-knowledge includes self-information that is held in our consciousness. At any given moment, your sense of self and identity are determined by your working self-concept or perceived self.

Your active self-conceptions are presently accessible in thought and memory, and can change depending on what you pay attention to, and are highly responsive to context, such as your social identity needs. Hazel Markus and Ziva Kunda, in their research on the malleability of the self-concept, noted that the person you perceive yourself to be when talking to your school principal or college professor is different to the person you perceive yourself to be when talking to your best friend.[4]

Something similar occurs if your social identity need for friendship is activated. For example, imagine that you have been away visiting your family in another country and you have been missing your friends back home. In that moment, you might perceive yourself to be a person who needs their friends around, and who does not like to spend too much time apart from them. Charles Carver and Michael Scheier, in their research into self-regulation, note that any momentary variation can lead to changes in motivations, thoughts and behaviours.[5]

Your social identity needs guide your future possible selves

Another term for your future self is your ideal or possible self. This represents the set of traits, competencies and values you would like to possess. In their research, Elanor Williams and Thomas Gilovich note that who we are is not just who we are right now or what we were like in the past, but also who we are striving to be.[6] Your hopes and dreams shed light on how you view yourself, as they express the type of person you want to become.

Many prominent developmental psychologists place the ideal self at the centre of their theories, for example in Albert Bandura's conception of personal standards.[7] Carl Rogers, building on the work of William James, described the ideal self as what the individual thinks he/she should be, and one's level of self-regard as a function of how far one is from their image of their ideal self.[8]

This is all very useful for your psychological toolkit. You don't have to anchor your view of yourself around negative self-perceptions. You are an active agent with the power to change how you think about yourself and to develop a positive, pragmatic way of seeing yourself. You can be proactive and make improvements where you see as necessary.

Describe what type of person you would like to become:

_____

_____

_____

_____

_____

Clearly creativity is involved, which you will get to explore in Chapter 10 of the workbook. What also becomes apparent is that your present self in any given moment communicates to your future self about your past self. This facilitates the feelings of continuity and stability that we feel with regard to who we are.

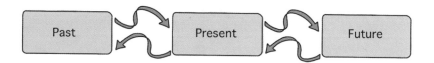

In the present moment, you utilise activated self-knowledge. This could be a past memory that has been retrieved from your long-term memory, and which can then be used to develop a plan for who you would like to become.

Try for yourself. Describe a time when your present self coordinated with your past and future selves.

Summary

What have you added to your psychological toolkit?

- You have considered your fundamental need for a positive view of yourself.

- You have learned about and explored three social identity needs: friendship and belonging; autonomy; and esteem needs, which will be the focus of Part 2.

- You have considered how these needs act as perceptual filters to your stored knowledge of yourself and motivation.

5 My Psychological Resources of Social Identification

 Your *social identity* is, very simply, how you think about yourself in relation to other people. In psychological terms, we would say it is your subjective or psychological conception of yourself in relation to others. Although a mouthful, you are becoming proficient in using this terminology.

Within psychology, many theorists have proposed that the self and identity are always socially created. This would suggest that the only real way to know who you are is in relation to others around you, for example through your social attachments, friendships, roles, relationships and group memberships.

Paul Ricoeur noted that 'the self is also other',[1] while Rom Harré stated that we exist for ourselves and for others.[2] Carl Rogers highlighted that our meaning-making depended on someone recognising us,[3] as did Edward Sampson when he proposed that 'the other endows us with meaning and clothes us in comprehension'.[4] This is also in line with William James, who noted that one 'has as many social selves as there are individuals who recognise' him / her,[5] which coincides with Charles Cooley's 'looking-glass self'[6] – our sense of self is our perception of how others evaluate us.

What will become apparent is that your personal meaning-making and identity work (that is, your construction and development of identity), only become psychologically real via comparison with others through *social embeddedness*.

In this chapter, you are going to:

- explore the interpersonal system of who you are;

- develop your understanding of how you make sense of who you are through social identification;

- construct models of who you are in terms of personal, collective and relational identities, and identifications.

Social embeddedness is really interesting; from the very first moments of life, infants demonstrate our social nature and the need for human connection. Newborns are innately sensitive to their mother's voice, and to voices around them. I am sure that you have all witnessed an infant crying who then stopped crying when they heard a voice talking to them. Maybe it was your voice?

A system of personal and social identities

We can organise and think about ourselves in terms of personal and social identities. We can make meaning in terms of how much a particular identity is independent or connected to others. In psychology, this is termed the level of *social inclusiveness*.

We are going to focus on three types of identities – *personal*, *collective* and *relational* – based on how socially connected or embedded they are. In later chapters, we will look at other identities such as our virtual identity or social media identity, which have developed among social media and smartphone users.

> Personal identity – self-categories which define you as unique and distinct from others. Also known as working self-concept.
>
> Collective identity – social categories which you believe you belong to, organised as group membership.
>
> Relational identity – social roles that you believe that you hold, organised as roles and relationships.

At any given moment, your sense of self and identity are determined by your personal identity or working self-concept. This is because this is the point that you believe that you act from and think from; you take your perspective from this anchor point. This is where you are organising your thoughts and making meaning from and is experienced as the continuity of your point of view; it is where your continuous sense of self arises from.

Below is an illustration of your self-system of collective and relational identities, with your working self-concept (personal identity) at the core.

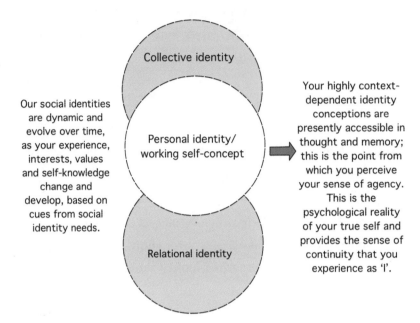

Our social identities are dynamic and evolve over time, as your experience, interests, values and self-knowledge change and develop, based on cues from social identity needs.

Collective identity

Personal identity/ working self-concept

Relational identity

Your highly context-dependent identity conceptions are presently accessible in thought and memory; this is the point from which you perceive your sense of agency. This is the psychological reality of your true self and provides the sense of continuity that you experience as 'I'.

When you are thinking about yourself either as a group member or in a role, your personal identity is also activated from this anchor point. Therefore, your personal identity is always implied.

Your personal, collective and relational identities overlap and are loosely fused together, combining to unite into a cohesive whole. You have a set of conceptions about yourself that are presently accessible in thought and memory, and this is the point from where you perceive your sense of agency. This idea of your personal identity coming to the fore reminds me of a toy: the magic eight ball. Your other fortunes are still there, but you are  focusing on the identity that is currently activated and accessible in your working memory or mental workspace. I have one caution about this metaphor of the eight ball, and that is that the current identity in focus has not surfaced out of chance; it has surfaced to the fore of your attention due to your activated social identity needs.

Personal identity/working self-concept

Let us look at our personal identity. We are all unique individuals. The meaning-making involved in the formation of personal identity involves defining ourselves in terms of interpersonal comparisons with others. That is, comparing our distinctiveness from others. We will look at collective identity and relational identity shortly. But first have a look at the following examples of personal identity statements or working self-concepts.

Does this idea of the working self-concept remind you of the concept of working memory we explored in Chapter 3?

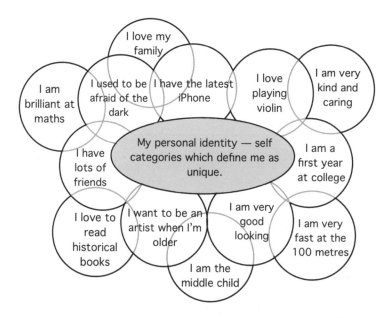

I love my family

I am brilliant at maths

I used to be afraid of the dark

I have the latest iPhone

I love playing violin

I am very kind and caring

I have lots of friends

My personal identity — self categories which define me as unique.

I am a first year at college

I love to read historical books

I want to be an artist when I'm older

I am very good looking

I am very fast at the 100 metres

I am the middle child

'I' fluctuates between your different personal identity positions. Whichever one is activated is where you are – where your 'I' is anchored during your thinking and meaning-making.

As you read through the collection of personal identity statements on the diagram above, you will notice that some are statements about hobbies and interests (e.g. *'I love playing violin'*). This is an example of how an interest is viewed as part of self and identity. Playing the violin is a very important enactment of identity in this statement – the person loves playing it. There are also personal identity statements illustrating values (*'I love to read historical books'*; *'I love my family'*). *'I am very good looking'* is an example of an identity judgement regarding one's physical appearance, while *'I am very fast at the 100 metres'* and *'I am brilliant at maths'* are judgements about the strengths and abilities one possesses.

Some personal identity statements refer to how a person considers themselves in the past, when they were younger (e.g. *'I used to be afraid of the dark'* – in this example, there has been a change to the self and now they are no longer scared of the dark). Personal identity statements referring to the past will require thinking back and delving into memory, as described in Chapter 3.

The way one hopes to be (e.g. *'I want to be an artist when I am older'*) is an example of an imagined future self. We also considered the important motivational elements of the future or ideal self in Chapter 4. There are also identity statements illustrating how ownership of an object can be fused with self and identity (*'I have the latest iPhone'*; *'I have lots of friends'*).

There are also statements that are relational (e.g. *'I am the middle child'* – being the middle child is a role embodied by the middle sibling in a family. I myself am a middle child, and it is often a salient role identity that I identify with, especially as I share this identity with both my husband and my son Oscar. We both identify with Oscar as the middle child, and have a shared understanding of what it is like to be in the middle) and one example of a collective identity statement: *'I am a first year at college'*. In college, this person is a member of the first-year student body.

Try one for yourself. What makes you different?

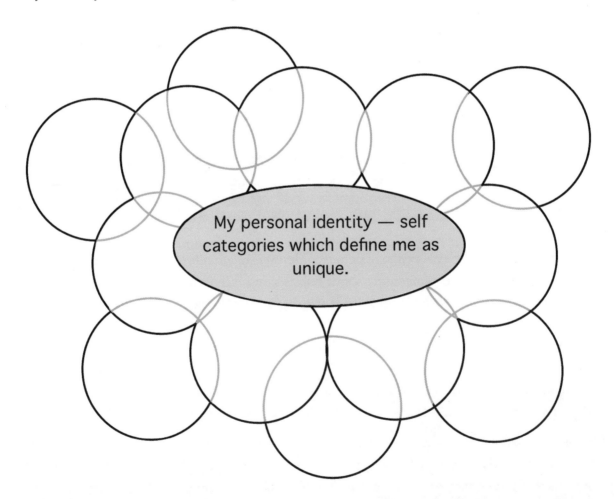

My personal identity — self categories which define me as unique.

Make a list describing each of your personal identity statements:

1.

2.

3.

4.

5.

6.

7.

8.

Social identification

Social identification is a very powerful identity resource; a way of thinking and organising our identities. It is a psychological orientation of the self in regard to something, for example behaviours, values, motives, roles or group memberships with a resulting feeling of emotions, specifically commitment and value.

Social identification – the act of identifying and committing to a particular identity.

With the cognitive process of identification, think about how much value you place on a particular identity, or how strongly you associate yourself with an identity.

You can use your self-questioning metacognitive skills. For example:

• Am I committed to this identity?

• Is it in line with my values?

Have a look at the following examples.

I identify very strongly with the values of my school for kindness and respect for one another, as I view myself as being kind and I value the importance of kindness in the world. I believe the world around us would be a far better place if everyone were kinder.

> Values of school in line with personal values.

I identify very strongly with my orchestra, as I view myself as a talented musician. We are like-minded and share experiences.

> The orchestra provides an opportunity to enact identity as a musician.

I do not identify with teenage violence, as I do not view myself as violent. I view myself as a peaceful person and I do not agree with teenagers physically hurting others.

> Teenage violence is not aligned with values, and therefore not identified with.

When I was younger, I loved to run around and race with my brothers. I loved to run as fast as I could. I began to see myself as a very fast runner. I loved when my family watched the Olympics track and field athletics. I loved to watch the 100m and 200m finals in particular to see who would win, and if any records would be broken. Looking back, I believe that I had such a good feeling about myself and enjoyed this so much because I saw myself as a fast runner and identified with these incredible athletes. Now I don't get the same level of enjoyment from it; I stopped competing when I was around sixteen and I no longer view myself as that fast.

> In this example, an individual in their twenties is thinking back on how much they enjoyed watching the Olympics as a child. You can see a change in how he views himself.

You will have noticed that the terms **identity** and **identification**, although related, are two different constructs. With regard to which comes first, identity emerges from the development of the self. As the self develops, this initially paves the way for the development of identity, and then of course the identity resource of identification can influence further development of the self.

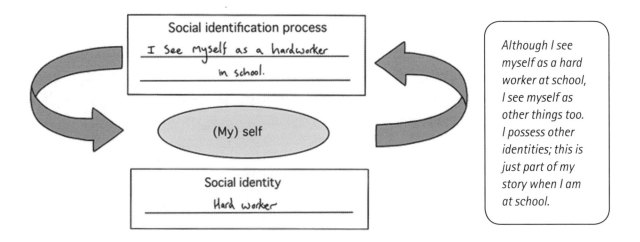

Why not try filling one out for yourself?

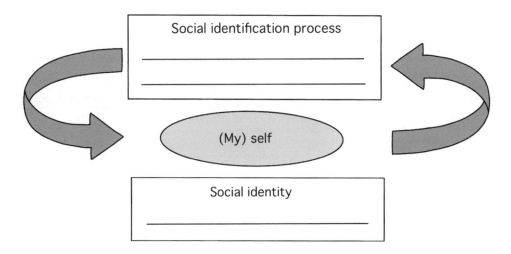

Another really interesting point here is that your portfolio of identities are really only partial identities; partial ideas of who you are. None of them hold the full picture of who you are.

Let's have another look at the identity statement above. In the example, the person might say 'I possess an identity as a hard worker, but I see myself as other things too. I possess other identities; this is just part of my story.'

Collective identity and identification (group membership)

We have already mentioned *collective identity* at the beginning of this chapter. It's where we think about our identity based on group membership. Collective identification is the meaning-making process by which we classify ourselves as a member of a group, and how important that membership is to us.

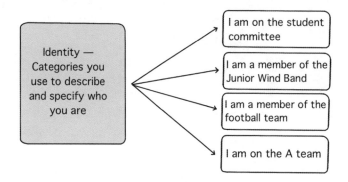

Think about the classification process for a moment. What you are actually doing is organising yourself into different social categories in order to create who you are, to form your self and identity. You are making sense and ordering the social environment in order to locate and define yourself in that environment.

Make a list of all the groups that you are a member of:

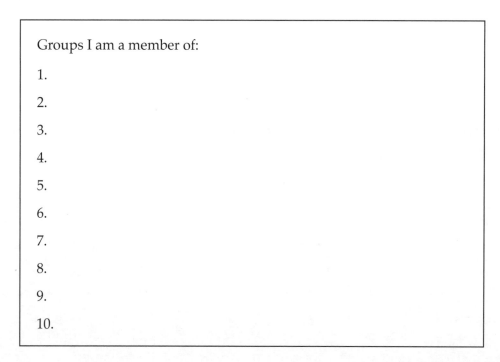

Groups I am a member of:

1.

2.

3.

4.

5.

6.

7.

8.

9.

10.

Think about each of these perspectives or group memberships for a moment.

- Do you think differently about yourself when you view yourself as a member of each group?

- How important is each group membership to you?

> Using the list that you have just created in the table above, fill in your four most important collective identities in the model below. This is your first model of your most significant collective identities.

Identity — Categories you use to describe and specify who you are	

> These identities are aspects of who you are – of your self-concept, your theory of your self derived from the social categories to which you see yourself belonging.

Think of the group membership (collective identity) that is the most important to you.

Why do you value this identity the most?

_____

_____

_____

_____

Why is your identification with this group the strongest?

_____

_____

_____

_____

_____

Do you have you the most interaction with this group?

Maybe you interact with this group daily.

> We often feel more part of groups that we interact with on a daily basis.

_____

_____

_____

_____

_____

What size is this group?

> In smaller groups, there is more opportunity for close contact communication, which presents you with opportunities to practise your identity, which will in turn strengthen your identification with it.

_____

_____

_____

_____

_____

Below shows how by using the self-work activity of collective identification and our meta-cognitive sense-making we can fulfil the social identity needs for friendship and belonging.

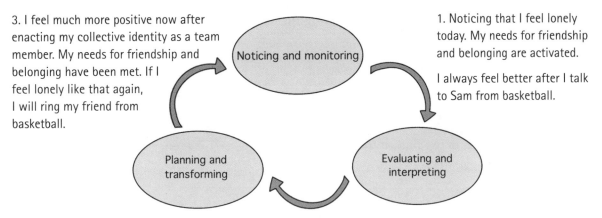

3. I feel much more positive now after enacting my collective identity as a team member. My needs for friendship and belonging have been met. If I feel lonely like that again, I will ring my friend from basketball.

Noticing and monitoring

1. Noticing that I feel lonely today. My needs for friendship and belonging are activated.

I always feel better after I talk to Sam from basketball.

Planning and transforming

Evaluating and interpreting

2. I identify with my friends from basketball. I value being a team member. I am going to ring my friend from my basketball team and talk about the upcoming game; this should cheer me up.

Collective identification is an identity resource for the fulfilment of your social identity needs as you strive for a positive sense of self and identity.

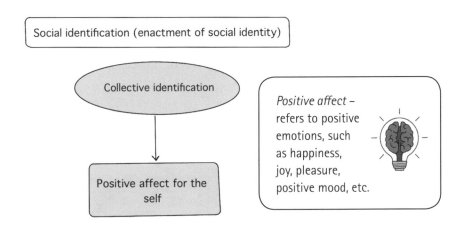

Social identification (enactment of social identity)

Collective identification

Positive affect for the self

Positive affect – refers to positive emotions, such as happiness, joy, pleasure, positive mood, etc.

There are numerous positive benefits that arise from your collective identifications. Collective identification offers you the psychological benefits of group membership. These include:

- A social connection – the positive feelings and emotions that develop from the strong affective bonds of attachment and belonging resulting from group membership. These increase wellbeing.

- The strong relationships among group members result in feelings of trust and feeling comfortable and at ease. This also produces a psychologically safe environment. (We will explore how important this is for creativity and resilience in Part 3 of this workbook.)

- Self-esteem from being part of the group, and also the self-esteem from aligning yourself with the values of others.

Relational identity and relational identification (roles)

We briefly looked at *relational identity* in our system of personal and social identities earlier in this chapter. This type of meaning-making involves identifying yourself in terms of your interpersonal relationships and role 'dyads', and the importance of the attachment bond. You make sense of yourself as an occupant of a role, and you also identify with the expectations associated with the role and its performance.

A role dyad is a type of relationship consisting of two people, for example:

Teacher – student   Mother – daughter

Father – son   Brother – sister

Here is an example taken from the model of a teenage girl giving her most significant relational identities:

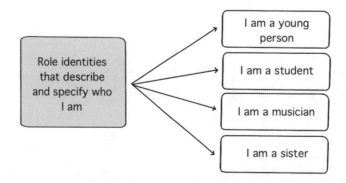

Try making a list of all the roles that you occupy:

Roles that I occupy:

1.

2.

3.

4.

5.

6.

7.

8.

9.

10.

Think about each of these perspectives or roles for a moment. Do you think differently about yourself when you view yourself in each role?

Think of your relationships with your friends and teachers. Do you notice any differences in your identity in these different relationships? How important is each role to you?

Bear in mind that it is perfectly normal to construct unique identities with different relationships and different group memberships. This is not being fickle or manipulative; your personal identity is still essentially the same, you are merely acting from a different perspective. All these different perspectives make up who your true self is; who you truly are.

Using the list that you have just created in the table above, fill in your four most important relational identities in the model below. This is your first model of your most significant role identities.

My first model of my most significant relational identities

These identities are aspects of (your) self-concept, your theory of (your) self derived from the social categories to which you see yourself belonging.

Role identities that describe and specify who I am

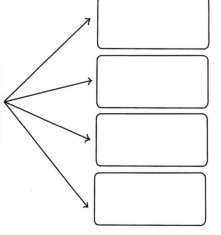

Early relationships are important in how information about who you are is organised. Children become part of the social order gradually, so at this stage in your life, you have probably built up a large number of relationships.

Let's explore how many social orders you are now part of:

Think of your earliest relationship, maybe it was with your parents or a sibling. Think about how it has changed over time.

Describe your earliest relationship – again you will notice that you are delving into your past here to make sense of your earliest memory.

_____

_____

_____

What is your most important relationship? Or what is your most important role?

_____

_____

_____

Why is it so important to you? Maybe you like who you are the most in this role, or maybe it is how you are around this particular person.

_____

_____

_____

How do you think that person views you?

_____

_____

_____

Below is an example showing how to use the self-work activity of relational identification and our metacognitive sense-making to fulfil the social identity need of self-esteem through enacting the role of a good mathematician.

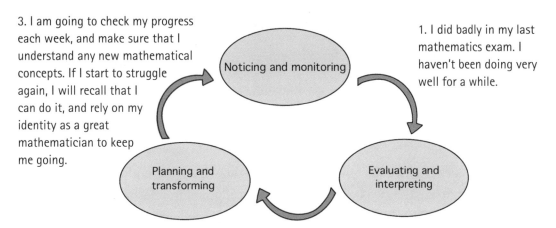

3. I am going to check my progress each week, and make sure that I understand any new mathematical concepts. If I start to struggle again, I will recall that I can do it, and rely on my identity as a great mathematician to keep me going.

1. I did badly in my last mathematics exam. I haven't been doing very well for a while.

Noticing and monitoring

Planning and transforming

Evaluating and interpreting

2. I am a really good mathematician. When I think about my role as a great problem solver, I remember all the mathematics tests that I have excelled in and how good that felt. I have a strong need to do well in mathematics in order to fulfil this need and increase my self-esteem, as I want to feel like that again.

Relational identification is an identity resource for the fulfilment of your social identity needs in your quest for a positive sense of self and identity.

```
┌─────────────────────────────────────────────┐
│       Social identification (enactment)       │
└─────────────────────────────────────────────┘

                ╭───────────────────╮
                │  Relational identity  │
                ╰───────────────────╯
                         │
                         ▼
               ┌──────────────────┐
               │ Positive affect for the │
               │        self        │
               └──────────────────┘
```

There are numerous positive benefits that arise from your relational identifications. These include:

- When you perform well in a role, this successful role verification and accomplishment results in feelings of mastery and competence, self-efficacy and self-esteem.

- Performing a role well also fulfils the need for autonomy, which again will lead to increases in your self-esteem.

- Your social identity needs for affiliation are also fulfilled through the sense of belonging that arises from occupying a position in the relationship.

> Your identity construction shows the malleability of your personal identity or working self-concept, and how easy it is to shift in and out of these constructions.

We noted at the very beginning of this chapter that who we are depends on our perception of how others evaluate us; that we become psychologically real in relation to others. Let's take some time to explore this a bit further.

Imagining how you are viewed by others

Describe how you think the following people think of you:

- Your parents/caregivers:

_____

_____

_____

- Your best friend:

_____

_____

_____

- Your sibling(s):

_____

_____

_____

- Your favourite teacher:

_____

_____

_____

- Your least favourite teacher:

_____

_____

_____

Do you act in accordance with how you think they view you?

_____

_____

_____

Do you think they have accurate views of you?

_____

_____

_____

Are any of these perceived views based on a particular incident?

_____

_____

_____

Read through the following statements and, for each item, select one of the response choices, and write the number for your choice in the space provided. Remember to answer as honestly and accurately as you can.

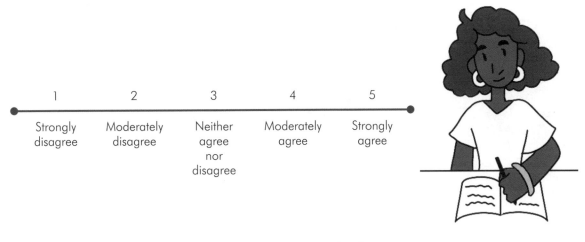

1. I often make decisions based on what others might think _____

2. It is important to me that others approve of my behaviour _____

Total score _____

Interpreting your results

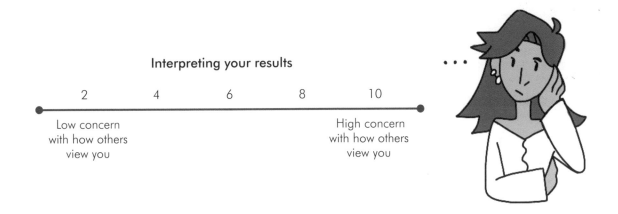

Reflecting on your evaluation

Is your concern for what others think of you high, moderate or low?

Are you surprised by your evaluation?

Although we have noted that our personal identity fluctuates between different identity positions, we can still feel somewhat stable. We have already touched on whether there is a feeling of being stable and continuous. You may be aware of this feeling, but you may not be able to define what it is. In order to illustrate the feeling of being continuous, due to the binding function of our personal identity, consider the following questions:

In relation to how you see yourself in your different groups and roles, does something remain the same?

Is that you?

_____

_____

_____

Are you the same person now as you were when you started school?

_____

_____

_____

Are you the same person now as you were two years ago?

_____

_____

_____

Is it through your memories that you are experiencing continuity?

_____

_____

_____

Is there some inner core of yourself that has remained the same? Can you describe what has remained the same?

_____

_____

_____

Or are you completely different? And if so, how?

_____

_____

_____

Consider both types of social identities for a moment. What are your most salient (important) identities?

_____

_____

_____

Where am I anchored?

A positive sense of self and identity are so important. The view that you adopt of yourself – your self-concept – affects how you interact with the world around you. It becomes your filter, and influences everything you do and believe in. It is the point which you think and act from. You are at the centre of every thought that you have, as the thinker. It is in fact your unique position, like an anchor point from which you navigate throughout your world. As Socrates is noted for proposing, 'to find yourself, think of yourself'.[7]

> ### LOCATION
>
> In *The Cultural Psychology of Self*, Ciarán Benson describes self as a locative system: 'Where and when, place and time, are the conditions of existence.'[8]
>
> When we refer to feeling lost inside, we mean that we have lost our anchor point or our perspective.
>
> We are always somewhere – even when we are lost, we are still somewhere, we just don't know where that somewhere is!

Summary

What have you added to your psychological toolkit?

- You have considered the interpersonal origins of how you come to know yourself.

- You have learned to think about yourself in terms of personal and social identities.

- You developed your own model of your multiple personal identities.

- You have learned your social identification processes.

- You constructed your first model of your collective identities, and one for your relational identities.

- You have answered questions based on your group memberships and roles.

- You considered what psychological resources arose from your collective and relational identifications.

- You have also considered the continuous and stable feeling of your self and identity.

PART 2

A CLOSER LOOK AT MY SOCIAL IDENTITY NEEDS

The aim of Part 2 is to tease out just how important the three social identity needs – affiliation (friendship and belonging), autonomy (control over decision-making) and esteem (self-esteem/pride and social status) – are for making sense of who you are. You will have the opportunity to actively see how fulfilling those needs through your social identifications enhances your positive sense of self and identity and your personal worth.

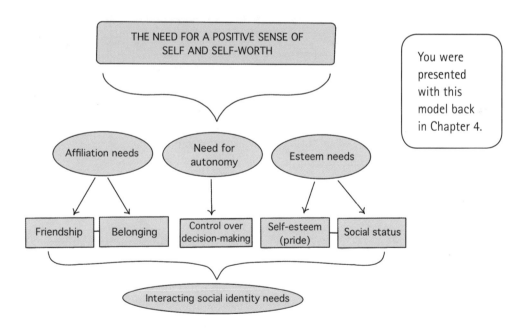

The following model sums up what you have explored in Part 1 in relation to the role played by your social identity needs, social identifications and your motivation. You can also apply the model as you progress through Parts 2 and 3 of the workbook.

Social identity needs

Affiliation: Friendship
                   Belonging

Autonomy: Competence
                Control over decision-making

Esteem: Social status and pride

Once a social identity need is activated or found wanting, you are then motivated to fulfil it.

motivating

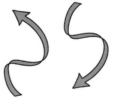

Social identifications

- **Collective identifications**
  Memberships:

  School, college, class, family, peer groups, sporting groups, etc.

- **Relational identifications**
  Role Identities:

  Child, sibling, cousin, mother, musician, teacher, athlete, friend, etc.

Your social identity needs are fulfilled by your collective and relational identifications.

fulfilled

Positive outcomes for self

Self-esteem, self-efficacy

Positive sense of self and wellbeing
Sense of belonging and acceptance
Emotional closeness, strengthened relational ties, liking and trust
Resilience, compassionate mind
Safe to make mistakes and take risks

You gain positive outcomes from the fulfilment of your social identity needs.

6 My Need for Friendship and Belonging

We can all agree that friendships enrich our lives in so many ways, and have a positive impact on our wellbeing. It is well established in the field of psychology that the affiliation needs for *friendship* and *belonging* are fundamental to our development and maintenance of a positive self and identity, and to our self-worth. In general, this refers to our motivation to be in close contact with others, and to be able to cooperate or reciprocate with friends and close contacts.

> *'A friend is someone who understands your past, believes in your future and accepts you just the way you are'* – author unknown
>
> I like this idea, as it represents the past, present and future self which we discussed in Chapter 4.

Psychologists such as John Bowlby[1] and Abraham Maslow,[2] often referred to as attachment theorists, believed that the degree of warmth and affection in our earliest relationships can make a critical difference in all aspects of our lives and wellbeing.

> In this chapter, you are going to:
>
> - explore and develop your understanding of your need for friendship and belonging;
>
> - explore the nature of friendship and the different types of friends you have;
>
> - practise using your self-work skills to create models of your affiliation needs.

Social identity needs for affiliation: friendship and belonging

One of the most central and fundamental influences on our behaviour has got to be the motivation for social contact. In 1938, Henry Murray defined the need for affiliation as 'to draw near and enjoyably cooperate or reciprocate with an allied other'.[3] Throughout this workbook, we are viewing the need for affiliation as being made up of two closely related constructs: the need for friendship and the need to belong.

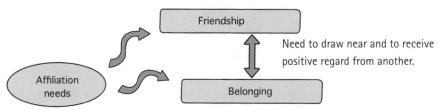

Friendship

Friendship is a relationship of mutual affection between people. This refers to a bond between people that connects them and allows them to share feelings, thoughts, fears and dreams. This friendship bond is a stronger type of interpersonal bond than with an acquaintance or an association with a neighbour, work colleague, classmate or member of the football team.

Below, you can explore some quotes from research I carried out with a group of medical staff in their early twenties. They were asked about the importance of their need for friendship.

'Friends can be of great help in times of real need . . . so friendship is really important.'

'We have to develop a friendly relationship with each other as we have to work as a team, and friendship and trust are very important.'

'If you don't have a good friendship, you won't feel like working in the place.'

'We work here as a team and so if the team is to succeed, we all have to work amicably.'

'In this kind of job, friendship, respect and the dignity of each person is very important.'

'If you work with friends, and you have some nice relationships instead of being enemies and fighting, of course it's easier.'

'For me, friendship and having people I can trust are the most important things because it's hard to do this job.'

'You always need someone to be there for you.'

'For me, it's the friendship that motivates you to work.'

It is clearly evident that these young adults had very salient friendship needs. You can see references made to friendship and trust, teamwork, nice relations and motivation.

Did anything strike you as unusual?

Do you agree or disagree with how the group responded?

Now that you have had the opportunity to explore how other young adults have made sense of their need for friendship, why not make some sense of your own?

Evaluating your need for friendship

Take a moment and think about your own need for friendship.

Read through the following statements and, for each item, select one of the response choices, and write the number for your choice in the space provided.

Remember to answer as honestly and accurately as you can.

1	2	3	4	5
Strongly disagree	Moderately disagree	Neither agree nor disagree	Moderately agree	Strongly agree

1. I like making friends with new people   _____

2. I like to be liked by others   _____

3. I believe that happiness equals lots of friends   _____

4. I try to be in the company of friends as much as I can   _____

5. I choose hobbies that involve other people   _____

6. I spend a lot of time texting/visiting my friends   _____

7. I love to get involved with group projects to meet new friends   _____

8. I go out of my way to meet new people   _____

9. I like to have a wide circle of friends   _____

10. I like to make as many friends as I can   _____

Total score   _____

Interpreting your results

10   20   30   40   50

Low need
for
friendship

High need
for
friendship

Reflecting on your evaluation

What have you learned about your need for friendship?

Is your friendship need high, moderate or low?

Are you surprised at how you evaluated this need?

Do you think you need to do more to satisfy your need for friendship or is it being fulfilled?

What could you do to fulfil this need?

Could you join another sporting group, or get more involved in your friendship roles?

Belonging

Like friendship, belonging is also fundamental to our sense of happiness and wellbeing. Belonging refers to our sense of fitting in, or feeling like you are an accepted member of a group. Belonging to what, one may ask? Basically, belonging to one another, to our friends and families, and also to our country and to our world. In Chapter 13, we will return to the need to belong to our community, country and the world itself.

> Below, you can explore some more quotes from the group of medical staff; this time they were asked about the importance of the need to belong.

'Unless I have a feeling of belonging, I will not be able to bring my best, so I am very committed to my work. That's because I do have that feeling that I belong.'

'I feel part of the team; that's what pushes me.'

'Yeah, it's very important, we need to belong. I'm not from this country, so I need belongingness from everybody around me and in my work to motivate me.'

'It is very important to have a sense of belonging because if you didn't feel like you belonged, you wouldn't want to come in every day.'

'Of course, it should be like family; you want to feel like you're needed here and you belong here.'

'That's why I love the word "belonging". Once you belong, and trust, teamwork will be there. Everything will develop as long as you belong inside the group.'

> The need to belong was so strong for this group. There were references again to trust, teamwork, friendship, family and motivation. I remember thinking at the time, wow, their need to belong is even more salient than the social connection element. It is this sense of belonging that has the more powerful emotional meaning for them.
>
> Did anything strike you as unusual?
>
> Do you agree or disagree with how the group responded?

Now that you have had the opportunity to explore how other young adults have made sense of their need to belong, why not make some sense of your own?

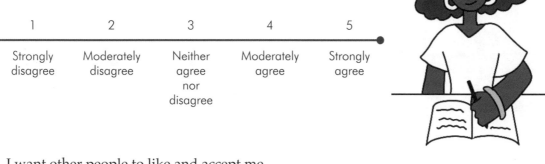

Evaluating your need for belonging

Take a moment and think about your own need for belonging.

Read through the following statements and, for each item, select one of the response choices, and write the number for your choice in the space provided.

Remember to answer as honestly and accurately as you can.

1	2	3	4	5
Strongly disagree	Moderately disagree	Neither agree nor disagree	Moderately agree	Strongly agree

1. I want other people to like and accept me   ____

2. I do not like being on my own   ____

3. It is important to me that I feel like I belong   ____

4. It bothers me when I am not included in other people's plans   ____

5. I need to feel that I have friends to turn to in times of need   ____

6. I do not like to work alone   ____

7. I do not like to be left out   ____

8. I need to feel part of the team   ____

9. I get upset if other people do not accept me   ____

10. I need to feel a connection with others   ____

Total score   ____

Interpreting your results

10	20	30	40	50

Low need
for
belonging

High need
for
belonging

Reflecting on your evaluation

What have you learned about your need to belong?

Is your need to belong high, moderate or low?

Are you surprised at how you evaluated this need?

Do you think you need to do more to satisfy your need to belong or is it being fulfilled?

What could you do to fulfil this need?

Could you join another sporting group, or get more involved in your friendship roles?

Have you got different types of friends?

Over the course of your life so far, you have probably made all sorts of friends.

For example you may have:

- childhood friends

- work friends

- school friends

- college friends

- friends from orchestra

- friends from football

- friends from down the street

You may also have friends that:

- you like to go shopping with

- you like to go running with

- live far away

- you see every day

- you see at the weekend

- you see a few times a year

Fill in the categories below with all your different types of friends. Some friends may end up in more than one group.

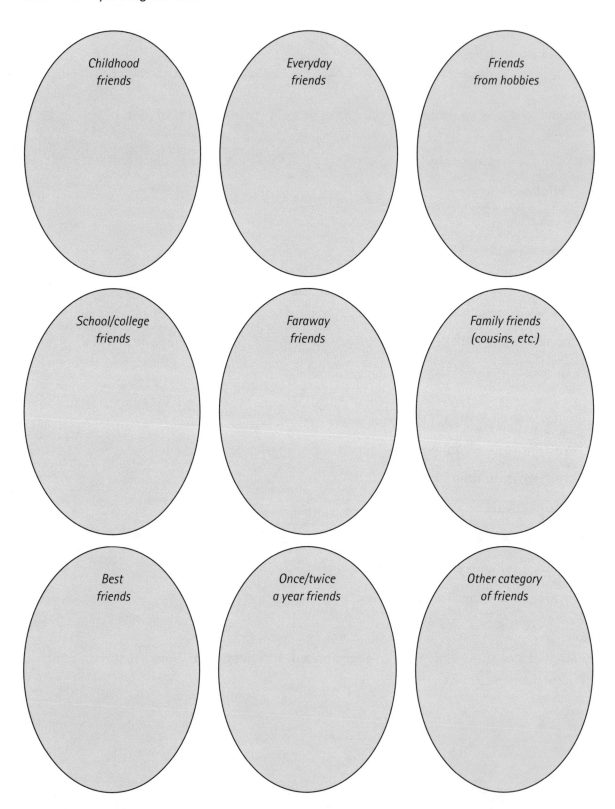

Childhood
friends

Everyday
friends

Friends
from hobbies

School/college
friends

Faraway
friends

Family friends
(cousins, etc.)

Best
friends

Once/twice
a year friends

Other category
of friends

What makes a good friend?

Have a look at the following list of personality traits that I believe a good friend possesses. I have given you a good start. See what you can add to the list based on what you value in a good friend.

- trustworthy   • caring
- honest   • empathetic
- dependable   • _____
- supportive   • _____
- funny   • _____
- non-judgemental   • _____
- good listener   • _____
- loyal   • _____

In reviewing the list above, choose and rank the five most important traits that you believe a good/best friend should possess.

1.

2.

3.

4.

5.

Does your best friend possess your top five traits for a good friend?

Here's another interesting question for you! Do your top five traits describe you?

_____

_____

_____

_____

After reflecting on what makes a good friend, and evaluating how you stand as a good friend, try the following question.

What can I do to become a better friend?

_____

_____

_____

_____

_____

Try to be honest and true to yourself. Remember that you never have to show your responses to anyone; they are for your own personal story.

Do we need close friendships?

I believe that we do; I do not believe that there is any other way to fulfil our social identity needs for affiliation.

Close friends are very important for positive wellbeing. These close connections are a powerful way for us to regulate our emotional distress.

For example, if you are in the company of someone you're securely attached to, it is an effective way to calm yourself down.

In a stressful situation, you might stay in neutral until you are with a loved one who can help you rehash and make sense of your experience.

A key to close friendship is intimacy; being able to be your true self and be seen and understood by others.

Reciprocation is key for a close friendship; you need to establish a psychological contract, where all members of the friendship group will feel seen and understood.

When you post something on Facebook and people give you affirmation in the way of nice comments or encouragement, that feels good but it doesn't necessarily create intimacy because there is no give and take.

Below is an example of a music student enacting their identity as a musician and orchestra member:

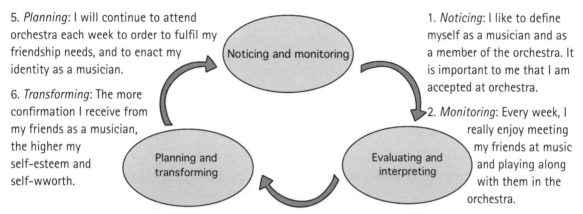

5. *Planning*: I will continue to attend orchestra each week to order to fulfil my friendship needs, and to enact my identity as a musician.

6. *Transforming*: The more confirmation I receive from my friends as a musician, the higher my self-esteem and self-wworth.

Noticing and monitoring

Planning and transforming

Evaluating and interpreting

1. *Noticing*: I like to define myself as a musician and as a member of the orchestra. It is important to me that I am accepted at orchestra.

2. *Monitoring*: Every week, I really enjoy meeting my friends at music and playing along with them in the orchestra.

3. *Evaluation*: I am enacting my valued identity as a musician and orchestra member. I feel that my friends like and accept me and I feel connected to them. I believe that my desire to be liked and accepted is being met. My motivation to be a member of the orchestra is also being met.

4. *Interpretation*: The feelings of closeness, belonging and acceptance arising from identifying as a musician and as an orchestra member allow me to feel good about myself, and increase my feeling of personal worth.

From the example above, you can see how you can apply your sense-making skills to determine if your friendship and belonging needs are being met through your identification with a valued identity. You can also figure out if the satisfaction that arises is improving your self-esteem and self-worth.

Try one yourself here:

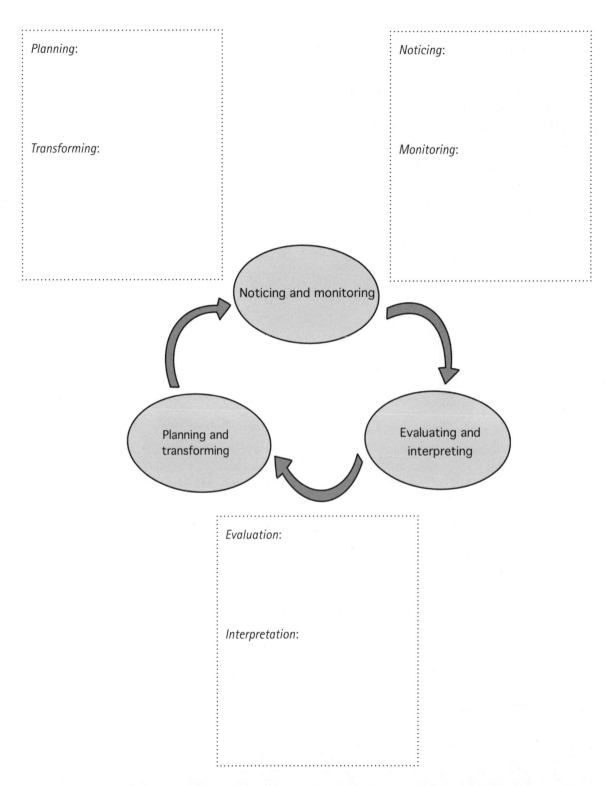

Planning:

Transforming:

Noticing:

Monitoring:

Evaluation:

Interpretation:

Noticing and monitoring

Evaluating and interpreting

Planning and transforming

You have already briefly explored whether your friendship and belonging needs are being met earlier in this chapter. You will find the following questions are useful to ask yourself:

1. Do the people I care about care about me too? _____

_____

2. Do I feel included in the groups that I am part of? _____

_____

3. Do I feel a close connection to my friends? _____

_____

4. Do I feel that those people I spend time with want to spend time with me too? _____

_____

5. Do I experience positive feelings when I spend time with those I feel connected to? _____

_____

6. Do I believe that my friends view me as a good friend? _____

_____

Frenemies

Frenemies refers to friends and peers who are actually mean to others. It is a mix of the words 'friends' and 'enemies'. Frenemies and toxic relationships are two types of social relationships which can lead pre-teens, teenagers, young adults and indeed older adults to feel bad about themselves. Anyone can fall victim to these types of negative relationships and experience an unhealthy friendship.

As opposed to fulfilling the social identity needs of friendship and belonging, these types of relationships can lead to you feeling bad about yourself, and can reduce your levels of self-esteem.

If you can tell what good friendships look like then you can be mindful of this, which can help you avoid toxic friendships.

Having a wide range of friends can also help you from relying on such negative friendships.

Ten signs of an unhealthy friendship:

1. The conversation is never equal; they spend most of the time talking and rarely listen to what you have to say.

2. They make fun of you or put you down in front of others.

3. You feel bad about yourself after you've spent time with them.

4. They talk about you behind your back.

5. They tell others things you have confided in them; you feel that you can't trust them with your secrets.

6. They exclude you from things with shared friends.

7. They let you down.

8. They are not happy for you when you have successes.

9. They are competitive towards you.

10. They only get in touch when they want something from you.

Reciprocation and mutual respect are very important for a good relationship.

What impact did the COVID crisis have on your friendships?

Maybe you adapted to using WhatsApp, Zoom calls, FaceTime.

Summary

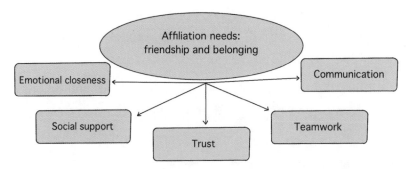

What have you added to your psychological toolkit?

Friends can enrich your life in many ways and have such a positive impact on your wellbeing:

- Having strong social ties and connections with your friends can decrease feelings of loneliness.

- You can ask your friends about things you are unsure about; they can act as social moral indicators. If they also believe that something you did was the right thing to do, that can help you make sense of your thoughts and behaviours.

- Friendships offer emotional support; they facilitate a healthy mood and happiness.

- Friendships can increase your sense of belonging and purpose, and offer support during hard times.

- You may have self-doubts and insecurities from time to time – having friends that support you can also play a big role in building your self-esteem.

- Having supportive friends can help you feel more supported and offer you a psychologically safe environment, where it is okay to make mistakes, which helps with your resilience. (We will return to this in Chapter 9.)

- As you connect with other people, you feel seen, known, valued and, very importantly, understood. This is confirmation of your image of yourself; of your self and identity!

Try making a list of the positive outcomes of having friends:

1.
2.
3.
4.
5.
6.
7.
8.

7 My Need for Autonomy

Jean-Paul Sartre, a very famous philosopher, believed that our way of being is linked to our choices. Sartre proposed that we are our choices; to be is to choose.[1] Going back to our model at the beginning of Part 2, the second social identity need considered important for the development and maintenance of a positive self and identity is the need for *autonomy*. Psychological theories of motivation have always stressed the importance of this for our wellbeing.

Back in the 1960s, Richard De Charms highlighted the importance of personal causation as the desire to be an 'origin' or initiator of your own behaviour rather than a pawn to external forces.[2] The key is to be a master of your own domain, as opposed to being a puppet on a string. Personal causation is similar to the concept of intrinsic motivation, which was loosely defined as behaviour performed for its own sake rather than for the purpose of acquiring any material or social rewards.

However, Edward Deci and Richard Ryan noted that there was more involved, and went on to describe intrinsically motivated behaviours as those which a person engages in to feel competent and self-determining.[3]

You can watch some YouTube videos in which Edward Deci describes his self-determination theory and views on motivation:

- 'Edward Deci – Self-Determination Theory'[4]

- 'Intrinsic Motivation with Dr Edward Deci'[5]

In this chapter, you are going to:

- explore the importance of making your own decisions, and having control over your life;

- evaluate your own social identity need for autonomy and develop a model of a time when you satisfied this need;

- explore the importance of satisfying your need for control for your self-esteem and self-efficacy.

Social identity need for autonomy

Autonomy refers to your growing ability to think, feel and make decisions and act on your own. During your pre-teen and teen years, this has had a special meaning for you because it signifies that you are a unique, capable, independent person, who depends less on parents and other adults. All the self-work that you have carried out so far will help you with making decisions and fulfilling your need for autonomy because a well-defined idea of who you are, a well-defined self, helps in making decisions.

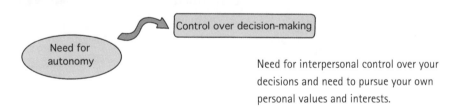

This need involves striving for interpersonal control over the decisions you make and the need to establish and maintain acceptable relations with others, and to be competent. It also involves the need to pursue your own personal values and interests, and to have personal control and self-determination, which all play a key role in your overall drive for positive self-worth and identity.

Below, you can explore some more quotes from my medical staff research. This time they were asked about the importance of the need for decision-making.

'Making decisions is very important.'

'Everybody has decision-making within their own level; the nurses in their level and the carers in their level. If they have any doubt, they can go to their seniors.'

'Yes it's very important. If you are clear what has to be done, then it is easier to make plans for the job so, for example, who has to be attended to first or second – who has to be fixed first.'

'Clinical decision-making regarding a resident and their medication needs to stay with the nurses. This is important for the nurses to feel good about their work, and their ability to make decisions about the welfare of the patients in their care. If you think that a patient needs urgent care at a hospital, then you need to be able to sanction this. If we can't, then this could frustrate the nurse as a decision-maker.'

It is clearly evident that these young adults had very salient needs for autonomy. You can see references made to decision-making and role identity.

Clearly in the final example, the nurse viewed this need as a fundamental part of her role identity, and felt that nurses would not feel good about their roles if they were unable to make decisions.

You could speculate that if her need for control over decision-making was not met, her role identification as a nurse would be negatively affected, resulting in a blow to her self-esteem and her sense of self-efficacy, and ultimately her fundamental sense of personal worth.

You can also see references made to friendship and trust, teamwork, nice relations and motivation.

When reading through the quotes, did anything strike you as unusual?

Do you agree or disagree with how they responded?

Evaluating your need for autonomy

Take a moment and think about your own need for autonomy.

Read through the following statements and, for each item, select one of the response choices, and write the number for your choice in the space provided.

Remember to answer as honestly and accurately as you can.

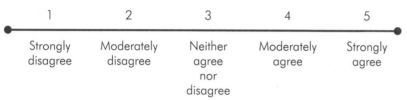

1	2	3	4	5
Strongly disagree	Moderately disagree	Neither agree nor disagree	Moderately agree	Strongly agree

1. I enjoy making my own choices _____

2. I believe in myself _____

3. I am confident in the decisions that I make _____

4. My decisions reflect what I really want _____

5. I believe that I will do well in the future _____

6. I feel capable in what I do in general _____

7. I have the freedom to choose what I will undertake _____

8. I believe that I can successfully complete difficult tasks _____

9. I believe that the choices I make express who I really am _____

10. I do things that really interest me _____

Total score _____

Interpreting your results

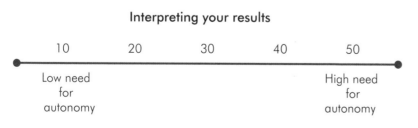

10	20	30	40	50
Low need for autonomy				High need for autonomy

Reflecting on your evaluation

What have you learned about your need for autonomy from filling out the self-questionnaire?

Is your need for autonomy high, moderate or low?

Are you surprised at how you evaluated this need?

Do you think you need to do more to satisfy your need for autonomy or is it being fulfilled?

What could you do to fulfil this need?

Below is an example of a student enacting his need for autonomy:

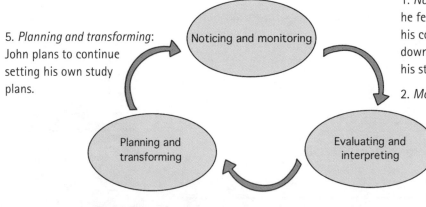

1. *Noticing*: John notices that he feels more in control of his college work when he sits down each week and organises his study schedule for himself.

2. *Monitoring*: Each week he gets more done during his scheduled study time, and feels motivated to get even more accomplished in each time slot.

5. *Planning and transforming*: John plans to continue setting his own study plans.

3. *Evaluation*: He recognises that he is enacting his need to be in control of his time. He has always liked to set his own rules, as opposed to being hampered by the rules and procedures of others.

4. *Interpretation*: He feels a strong sense of mastery and self-efficacy when he is in control of his own schedule.

From the example, you can see how you can apply your sense-making skills to determine if your need for autonomy is being met through your identification with a valued identity. You can also explore if the satisfaction that arises is improving your self-esteem and self-worth.

Try this now for yourself:

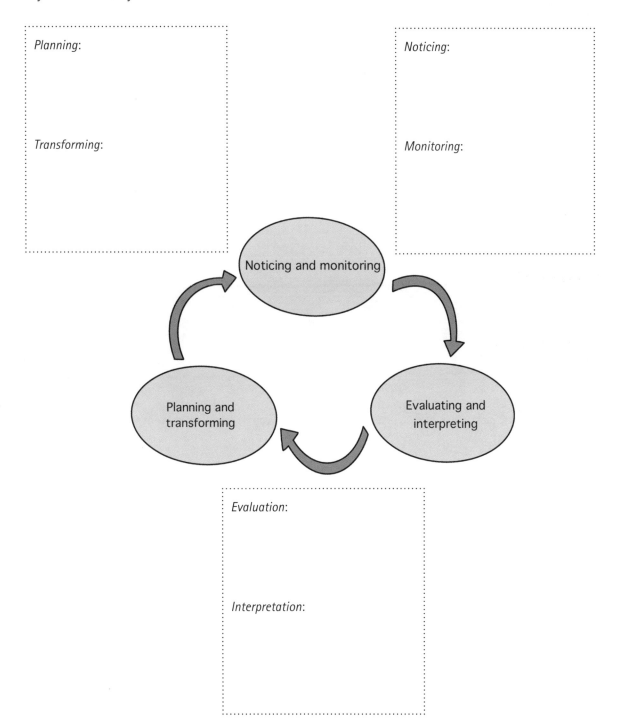

Planning:

Transforming:

Noticing:

Monitoring:

Noticing and monitoring

Planning and transforming

Evaluating and interpreting

Evaluation:

Interpretation:

When you exercise control over your decisions, and choose to pursue goals that are consistent with your values, you are being true to yourself. You are being authentic!

The following questions will guide you in your evaluation of whether your need for autonomy is being met:

1. Do believe that your behaviours and goals reflect your values?

_____

_____

_____

2. Do you continue to pursue your goals even if someone criticises you?

_____

_____

_____

3. Do you spend most of your time pursuing your goals or do you do what you think others expect from you?

_____

_____

_____

4. Are you aware of it when you are not behaving in a way that is consistent with your true self?

_____

_____

_____

Summary

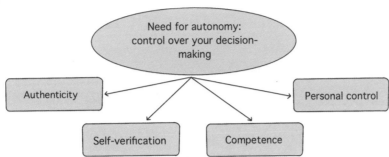

What have you added to your psychological toolkit?

- Being in control of your decision-making provides you with a sense of mastery, and a positive evaluation of yourself.

- Choosing your own goals that are aligned with your values enables you to be true to yourself, and increases feelings of being authentic.

- Being in control also helps you carry out your valued roles, feel a positive sense of accomplishment, and increases your feelings of self-esteem and self-efficacy.

Try making a list of some of the positive outcomes of being in control of your decision-making:

1.	
2.	
3.	
4.	
5.	
6.	
7.	
8.	

8 My Need for Self-Esteem

Through my extensive research in the area of self and identity and of the motivational self, it is clearly evident that our most fundamental motivation is toward increasing our self-esteem. This is more pervasive than any other self-motivation drive. Three prominent organisational researchers, Edwin Locke, Kyle McClear and Don Knight, noted that 'self-esteem is a profound state of mind, and that we could not tolerate the idea that we are fundamentally no good'.[1] (You might remember that I introduced this idea to you back in Chapter 4.)

A strong sense of self and self-concept are paramount for our self-esteem motive. As the sociologist Viktor Gecas described, the self-esteem motive is the motivation to maintain and enhance a positive conception of oneself.[2] The more positive our sense of self, the more motivated we are to preserve it, and also to increase the positive psychological resources that arise from increases in our self-esteem.

> In this chapter, you are going to:
>
> - explore the different ways self-esteem has been conceptualised;
>
> - evaluate some research on the motive of self-esteem;
>
> - evaluate your own need for self-esteem;
>
> - try some self-affirmations for an extra confidence boost;
>
> - consider how much you value physical appearance in assessing your worth.

Brief historical backdrop of self-esteem

Research into self-esteem has yielded a huge theoretical knowledge base, which has also meant that the term self-esteem is used in different ways by different researchers. (You might remember that we mentioned this phenomenon in the Welcome chapter, where we looked at science and psychology.) It can be useful to view this body of research from three perspectives.

1. Self-esteem has been studied as a global personality trait. From this perspective, self-esteem is viewed as a stable and enduring aspect of one's personality. It represents how you generally feel about yourself, as your overall sense of self-worth.

> Think of someone that you know who you would describe as having high self-esteem. Describe what it is about that person that has led to your judgement that they have high self-esteem. (Maybe they brag about their abilities, or maybe it is the confidence that they express.)
>
> _____
>
> _____
>
> Think of someone that you know who you would describe as having low self-esteem. Describe what it is about that person that has led to your judgement. (Maybe they express self-doubt or maybe they criticise themselves.)
>
> _____
>
> _____

2. The second area, self-esteem as a state, focuses on feelings and emotions of self-worth. State self-esteem is more fluid and temporary, and is based on your emotional reactions to things in your life. From this perspective, you can see how fulfilling your social identity needs could boost your state self-esteem.

> For example:
>
> *   John felt very proud of himself when he won the 200 metres hurdles at national level. He views himself as being a great athlete (role identification), so this accomplishment allowed him to enact and confirm that identity. His self-esteem was very high after winning the event.
>
> *   Susan felt ashamed after she was caught cheating in her science exam. She valued being a member of Science Club (collective identification), and now they all know that she has cheated. This violates her view of herself and has led to lower self-esteem.

3. The third approach investigates our domain specific self-evaluations of high and low self-esteem. You may feel that you have a great musical talent or maybe you are a sporting genius.

Rate your ability as high, moderate or low in the following domains:

Athletics	High, Moderate, Low
Football	High, Moderate, Low
Music	High, Moderate, Low
Creative writing	High, Moderate, Low
Drawing	High, Moderate, Low
Dancing	High, Moderate, Low

You will be focusing on your self-esteem as a motive; as the motivation to maintain and enhance a positive conception of our selves. You have already considered that you have a fundamental drive to maintain and increase your self-esteem in order to feel good about yourself. The need for esteem can be further divided into the need for self-esteem or pride and the need for social status, as seen in the figure below.

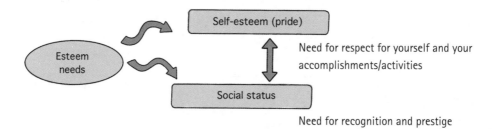

Self-esteem (pride in yourself)

> Below, you can explore some answers medical staff gave when they were asked about the importance of the need for self-esteem (pride).

'When you do your best, somewhere deep inside you want to be getting esteem – self-esteem.'

'The need for self-esteem is important; in order to think that you are good at what you do, you need to be respected yourself.'

'In my job, what motivates me is my pride. In my family, it is considered important to do your job as well as you can.'

'The quality of the job that you put in reflects you, so you need to have a sense of pride.'

'I feel great, I feel actually proud I'm a care assistant – this job has changed me.'

'Just to know that you're helping somebody and that you're putting their needs before yours gives job satisfaction, and I take pride in what I do and probably achieve something.'

It is clearly evident that these young adults had very salient needs for self-esteem (pride). You can see references made to having a sense of pride in carrying out work well and feeling good about doing a good job.

One of the care assistants described her need for self-esteem as stemming from the values within her family, which she shared. This need to be proud of her work was a significant part of her identity and sense of self at work, but she also viewed it as part of her identity within her family, and it was therefore a very strongly activated need for her.

You can also see the link between self-esteem and successful role verification in the quotes.

Did anything strike you as unusual from these responses?

Do you agree or disagree with how the group responded?

Self-esteem (social status)

The need for social status is defined as the need for recognition and prestige.

> This time the medical staff were asked about the importance of the need for social status. Here are some of their answers:

'It's not like a social status thing.'

'I find many times I have no motivation because I felt they didn't appreciate the work I do.'

'You work hard, so you want to be appreciated, and gain status among your peers.'

'It is important to be recognised by management.'

'I feel good about myself when the patient respects my position too.'

> Although the theme of social status has been proposed to be interrelated to the self-esteem need, a different trend emerged from the focus group data of the medical staff we have been exploring. The nursing home staff did not believe that the need for social status was as important as the need for self-esteem. The team-based working environment and the caring roles occupied by participants meant that the need for social status was not an activated need. This is really interesting, as you can see the role played by the environment.

> There was disagreement throughout the focus groups with the medical staff on the importance of the need for social status. Another care assistant noted that she often found that she had no motivation because she felt that her hard work had gone unappreciated by the management. The need for self-esteem was very important for her sense of self-worth, so when she felt that she was not appreciated, it directly affected her levels of motivation. The extract below presents some shared meaning-making that took place in one of the focus groups.
>
> JE: *Is it important to you to have self-esteem and social status needs, or the need for pride?*
>
> P1   *Self-esteem rather than pride, yeah.*

P2   *Both of them are needed I think. We have to have pride in ourselves because we are accomplishing things on a daily basis, I think.*

P3   *Social status and what type of qualification we have are important to me, actually.*

Participants 1 and 2 shared the view that the need for self-esteem and pride were important, however participant 3 held a divergent view. He felt that social status and qualifications were important. Participant 3 was a senior physiotherapist, who appeared to have incorporated his achievements and social status into his sense of identity at work. His educational qualifications, which were different from those of the care assistants and nursing staff, may have resulted in feelings of distinctiveness and uniqueness which would have increased his sense of self-worth.

All in all, with regard to the importance of the social identity need for social status, there was disagreement on how important the need was, although the general consensus was that it was not as important as the self-esteem need.

Did anything strike you as unusual?

Do you agree or disagree with how the group responded?

Are you motivated to be popular in school or university?

Popularity is often a very salient motive for students. Recall what you have already learned about your affiliation needs in Chapter 6. You can see how they can interact with your self-esteem needs.

> Evaluating your need for self-esteem

Take a moment and think about your own need for self-esteem.

Read through the following statements and, for each item, select one of the response choices, and write the number for your choice in the space provided.

Remember to answer as honestly and accurately as you can.

1	2	3	4	5
Strongly disagree	Moderately disagree	Neither agree nor disagree	Moderately agree	Strongly agree

1. My evaluation of my self-esteem as a personality characteristic

1. I feel that I have a lot of strengths   _____

2. I am able to do most things well   _____

3. I have a lot of respect for myself   _____

4. I rarely feel that I am a failure   _____

5. In general, I am happy with who I am   _____

6. I have a positive view of myself   _____

7. I think that others value me   _____

8. I feel that I have a lot to offer   _____

9. I rarely disappoint myself   _____

10. I believe that I am respected by others   _____

Total score   _____

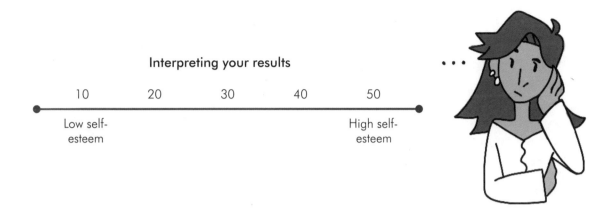

Interpreting your results

10	20	30	40	50

Low self-esteem

High self-esteem

2. My evaluation of my self-esteem motive

1. I like to do things well in order to increase my confidence   _____

2. I am concerned about my reputation and position in my social groups   _____

3. I like to be in charge   _____

4. I like to do better than others   _____

5. Status symbols are important to me   _____

6. I am motivated to be good at most things that I set my mind to   _____

Total score   _____

Interpreting your results

6	12	18	24	30

Low self-esteem motive

High self-esteem motive

Reflecting on your evaluations

What have you learned about your need for self-esteem from filling out the self-questionnaires?

Is your need for self-esteem high, moderate or low?

Are you surprised at how you evaluated this need?

Do you think you need to do more to satisfy your need for self-esteem, or is it being fulfilled?

What could you do to fulfil this need?

Self-affirmations are necessary for a continued self-esteem. You don't have to wait for affirmations from others; you can practise reciting self-affirmations to give yourself an extra confidence boost. Here are a few examples:

• I am loved

• I have lots of friends

• I am not afraid to fail

• I can easily make friends

• I can do what I set my mind to

• I am not afraid to ask others for help

• I am intelligent

• I love to try new things

Physical appearance and self-esteem

Physical appearance and self-esteem are often closely related. Your perception of how you look can have a big impact on the value that you place on yourself, and how much self-confidence you have in your day-to-day life. Your self-esteem can therefore depend on how much you believe physical appearance is important.

Below is an example of a student enacting his need for self-esteem:

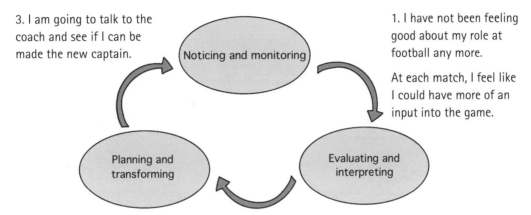

3. I am going to talk to the coach and see if I can be made the new captain.

1. I have not been feeling good about my role at football any more.

At each match, I feel like I could have more of an input into the game.

2. My need for social status is not being met. I think if I was made the captain of the team, I would feel much better about myself and I would be more motivated to play to a higher level.

Try one yourself here:

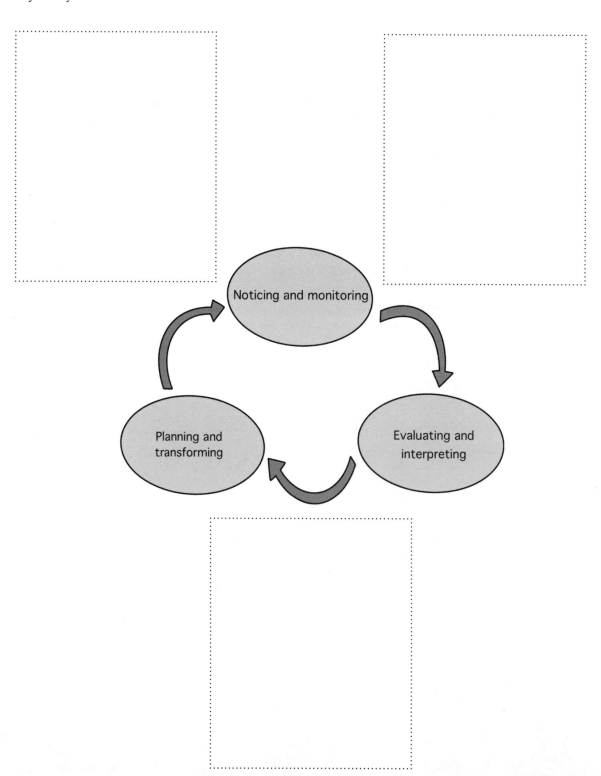

The following questions will guide you in your evaluation of whether your need for self-esteem is being met:

1. Do you believe that your behaviours are directed towards feeling good about yourself?

_____

_____

_____

2. Do you feel that you face life with confidence and a positive attitude, even if you make some mistakes?

_____

_____

_____

3. Do you spend most of your time pursuing goals that you know you can succeed at?

_____

_____

_____

4. Do you spend a lot of time pursuing challenging goals even when you are uncertain if you can succeed?

_____

_____

_____

Summary

There is a lot to say about this focal social identity need for self-esteem; to feel good about yourself, to feel that you have worth. At the beginning of Chapter 4, you explored the main findings that I felt were useful for you from the vast knowledge base of motivation. It was clear our behaviours are directed towards feeling good about ourselves, and many of the universal statements posed to you involved increased self-esteem as the end goal.

The three groups of social identity needs interact with each other, with self-esteem acting as a drive – directing behaviour but also as an end goal in itself.

Fulfilment of social identity needs through collective and relational identifications lead to the following positive benefits:

> **POSITIVE OUTCOMES FOR SELF**
>
> **Self-esteem, self-efficacy**
>
> Positive sense of self and wellbeing
>
> Sense of belonging and acceptance
>
> Emotional closeness, strengthened relational ties, liking and trust
>
> Resilience, compassionate mind
>
> Safe to make mistakes and take risks

What have you added to your psychological toolkit?

- Self-esteem allows you to face life with more confidence and optimism.

- Finding something that you are good at and feeling successful at something; this successful role accomplishment and enactment helps you feel good about yourself.

- This self-efficacy, this confidence and feeling of self-assurance, based on awareness and appreciation of your abilities, also increases your self-esteem and sense of worth.

- Feelings of pride from enacting your roles successfully enhance your positive conception of yourself.

PART 3

USING MY PSYCHOLOGICAL TOOLKIT

The aim of Part 3 is to present you with opportunities to apply the metacognitive and self-work skills that you have developed in your psychological toolkit to your daily life. The chapters in this section highlight how you can use your newly acquired skills to become more resilient and to deal with difficult and challenging situations.

You will see how much you can benefit from a flexible mindset in order to be creative and to express yourself creatively. These new skills also facilitate a more mindful and grateful approach to your sense-making. You will also have the opportunity to consider your role in society, and to consider how you can navigate more effectively in the technological world of today.

The ultimate goal of course is to apply your psychological toolkit to improve and maintain a positive sense of self and wellbeing.

9 My Resilient Self

The ideas put forward in this chapter are so important in the twenty-first century, where adaptability, resilience and learning agility are aligned with a positive sense of self and mental health. It is your reaction to failure and disappointment, not the failure and disappointment itself, that will determine how your life's story will develop.

In this chapter, you are going to:

- explore the concept of resilience, and how you have already developed psychological resources in your toolkit to deal with difficult and challenging situations;

- describe a situation where your flexible mindset increased your resilience;

- explore mental flexibility with the Wisconsin Card Sorting Test;

- apply your own self-system of multiple identities as a strategy to improve your resilience;

- consider how being comfortable with contradictory identities facilitates your resilience;

- explore the importance of being comfortable making mistakes;

- evaluate your resilience.

What is resilience?

In a nutshell, *resilience* refers to your ability to cope with a crisis or difficult situation, and your ability to return to pre-crisis status, or back to your usual self afterwards. A lot of people would claim that they actually feel stronger, wiser or more grateful afterwards, so there appears to be identity growth after overcoming the difficult situation. Ernest Hemingway, in *A Farewell to Arms*, described this strength when he wrote: 'The world breaks everyone and afterward many are strong at the broken places.'[1] Disappointments such as having your hopes, dreams and goals dashed are an inevitable part of life.

> Luckily for you, you have become more and more resilient as you have progressed through all the self-work activities in this workbook. The psychological toolkit that you have developed is invaluable here in developing strategies to be more resilient.
>
> We will look at how you can cash in on having multiple identities, and the psychological safety experienced from the fulfilment of friendship and belonging needs. The psychologically safe environment also facilitates taking risks and making mistakes without viewing them as violations of your social identities.

The ability to stay on track is an asset, but being stuck in the track is not! The type of identity clarity in focus here involves having a flexible mindset. You need clarity regarding the feelings of stability that arise from your personal identity, but you also need to be clear that your personal identities are malleable. This malleability enables you to be flexible and to navigate between multiple identities.

The feeling of stability arising from your personal identity, which is at the core of who you feel you are, gives you that sense of personal continuity. Remember that this sense gives you an anchor point which keeps that feeling of who you are present while you navigate between your multiple identities.

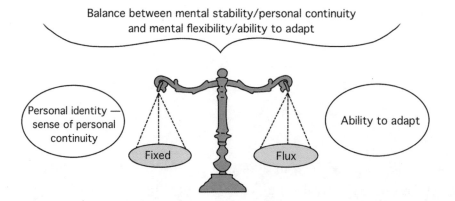

Balance between mental stability/personal continuity
and mental flexibility/ability to adapt

Personal identity — sense of personal continuity

Fixed

Flux

Ability to adapt

Sometimes we can suffer because we hold tightly to a fixed view of our self. No matter how focused we are on an activity or a thought, there comes a time when the situation calls for something else. Being able to change one's mindset is as important as staying mentally on track.

Switching with ease from one idea or social identity to another can appear like a natural ability. However it does require the complex neural machinery of the frontal lobes, which you considered in Chapter 2.

Recall Aaron Beck and his contributions to cognitive behavioural therapy. You explored how you can change your view of yourself by learning to question and challenge your own thoughts. By focusing on specific cognitive biases and problematic thought patterns, you can restructure to a more positive mindset.

Initial identity statement: I am no good at soccer. Restructure: I only started to play soccer a couple of weeks ago. I am improving every week. Before long, I will be a competent player.

Initial identity statement: I am terrible at mathematics. Restructure: What we are covering at the moment is difficult. With some practice, I should be able to understand. I can't be brilliant at everything, but I can certainly improve. I have other strengths.

Being mindful of the environment, of the difficult topic and of other personal strengths.

Describe a situation where your flexible mindset helped you to adapt in a difficult situation.

Mental flexibility also relies on creativity, which you will explore in the next chapter.

Wisconsin Card Sorting Test (WCST)[2]

This is a neuropsychological test which was initially developed to assess the ability to shift cognitive strategies in response to changes in situation. It is also considered a measure of executive functions.

In the original version of this test, a number of stimulus cards are presented to the participant. The participant is told to match the cards, but not *how* to match them. Instead, they are told whether a particular match is right or wrong. Once the participant has figured out the matching rule (based on colour, shape or number of objects, for example) and becomes fluent and comfortable using the rule, then the rule changes again.

The task requires guidance by internal representation, mental flexibility and working memory. (You can find a free online version and try it for yourself.)

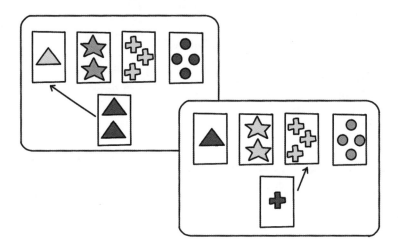

This test is useful for assessing mental flexibility and the ability to see things in a new light, which of course involves creativity and original thinking. We could therefore have looked at this test in Chapter 10, which focuses on creativity. However, we will focus on it here as it gives a great insight into cognitive flexibility during rule uncertainty. An example of rule uncertainty might be a stressful situation in which you need to be able to cope with changing rules, and which involves both mental flexibility and the cognitive persistence to keep trying until the new rules are understood.

Having a resilient mindset involves utilising your meta-competencies of identity growth and adaptability for positive self and identity.

Multiple identities

In Chapter 5, you developed your self-system of multiple identities. This is also a very useful intervention for improving your resilience. By identifying with numerous groups and/or occupying multiple roles, you develop a more resilient self and identity. Having your backdrop of multiple

identities helps you to become more flexible with your self-view and more able to adapt to a different self-identity in order to recover quickly from violations of your self-concepts, as in the example below:

Adam identified very strongly with his identity as a brilliant violin player. He competed in a national music competition, and really thought he might win. Unfortunately, he got so nervous that he made a lot of mistakes. Adam was not placed in the competition, and was really disappointed as he had worked all year towards this goal. His identity as a great violin player had been violated, as the situation did not confirm that he was a great player.

Initially, Adam felt worthless and his self-esteem was negatively affected. Then he sat down and made a list of all the things that he was really good at. For example, he also identified with being a great singer. His self-worth increased when he thought about how beautifully he had sung a solo part he had been given in a recent concert. Shifting his perspective to his identity as a singer allowed him to overcome the negative feelings he felt due to the violin competition. He began to feel more optimistic again about his violin playing and decided that there was always next year – he would compete again with another great year of practice behind him.

The malleability of the working self-concept and how you can engage different identifications, both relational and collective, is so useful for accommodating changes and disappointments in life more easily. Being comfortable in calling forth multiple identities, which are well defined and can be enacted with confidence, means that you will experience little anxiety or difficulty with being able to adapt.

Contradictory self-concepts/identities

Identity clarity also involves being aware of your multifaceted and potentially contradictory self-concepts/identities. *Functional flexibility* is a term often used to refer to being confident in your ability to call into play multiple, even contradictory ideas of yourself. *Functional fixedness* is the opposite end of this construct, where you can't imagine yourself in different roles.

- Think of a situation where you were introverted and one where you were extroverted.

    What in the situation called for you to be an introvert?

    What in the situation called for you to be an extrovert?

- Think of a situation where you were lazy, and one where you were very motivated.

    What in the situation led you to be lazy?

    What in the situation motivated you?

- Think of a situation where you were warm and caring towards someone and one where you were very cold.

    What in the situation led you to be warm and caring?

    What in the situation led you to be cold?

Paula dislikes her mathematics teacher. She does not identify with her at all, but she still enjoys the subject. She is intrinsically motivated to work hard at mathematics; she loves it. She also has a very salient goal to become an engineer when she is older because it involves mathematics.

Failing forward and identity growth

Failures can be painful experiences – they can certainly be defining moments in your life – but the failure does not define you.

Think of a time when you failed at something. This could have been a test or forgetting your lines in the school play.

You are the same person now as you were before the failure. Your sense of continuity remains; you are still all the great things that you have achieved.

Self-work: Reflect on the situation and learn from it to become stronger.

How does knowledge of failure impact on your sense of self?

_____

_____

_____

You can reflect on the other things that you are good at.

Remember you are still the same person before and after a failure. You can grow and become stronger; this is what is meant by failing forward.

Learning agility is another great idea. This is your ability to comprehend, to understand and benefit from experience, whether the experience is a success or a failure. This is something that you can now do with ease by utilising your psychological toolkit.

Imagine that your friend has been unsuccessful at something, and they are very disappointed.

How would you console them?

_____

_____

What advice would you give them?

_____

_____

Why not apply this advice to yourself the next time you find yourself in a similar situation?

_____

_____

Evaluating your resilience

Take a moment and think about your resilience.

Read through the following statements and, for each item, select one of the response choices, and write the number for your choice in the space provided.

Remember to answer as honestly and accurately as you can.

1	2	3	4	5
Strongly disagree	Moderately disagree	Neither agree nor disagree	Moderately agree	Strongly agree

1. I can deal with whatever life has to throw at me _____

2. I am able to adapt to changes as they occur _____

3. I can stay calm and focused when under pressure _____

4. It does not take me long to bounce back after a stressful event _____

5. Even when things are tough, I can continue to move forward _____

6. I am able to deal with feelings such as sadness, anger and fear _____

7. When I look back on my life so far, I can accept my failures without feeling like I am a failure _____

8. I am able to talk myself out of negative thought patterns when under pressure _____

9. I do not allow my worries to overwhelm me _____

10. I am able to cope with difficult times as I have experienced difficult times before _____

11. My self-belief gets me through difficult times _____

12. I do not avoid difficult tasks; I face them head on _____

13. I feel hopeful and optimistic even when I make a mistake _____

Total score _____

Interpreting your results

13   26   39   52   65

Low resilience

High resilience

Reflecting on your evaluation

What have you learned about your resilience?

Is your level of resilience high, moderate or low?

Are you surprised at how you evaluated your resilience?

Do you think you could do more to increase your level of resilience?

What could you do to increase it?

Summary

> **Fulfilment of social identity needs**
>
> Affiliation, Autonomy and Esteem
>
> _____
>
> **Collective and relational identifications**
>
> Multiple identifications
>
> Flexible mindset
>
> _____
>
> **Positive outcomes for self**
>
> Self-esteem, self-efficacy
>
> Positive sense of self and wellbeing
>
> Sense of belonging and acceptance
>
> Emotional closeness, strengthened relational ties, liking and trust
>
> Resilience, a compassionate mind
>
> Feel safe to make mistakes and take risks
>
> _____
>
> **Increased resilience**

What have you added to your psychological toolkit?

- Multiple identifications with different roles and groups can facilitate positive development and construction of your resilient, positive self and identity. Using the positive resources from your social identity need fulfilment leads to positive self-esteem and positive affect, which facilitate your resilience.

- Friendship increases emotional closeness and trust facilitates a psychologically safe environment where you can make mistakes and take risks.

10   My Creative Self

You are under no obligation to be the same person today that you were a year ago, or even a day ago! You have the right and ability to grow and develop, and to change things about yourself that you are unhappy about. Remember, your mindset consists of beliefs that are in your mind, and of course you can change your mind!

As the philosopher Georg Wilhelm Freidrich Hegel postulated, we are always engaged in ever-progressive motion; in giving ourselves a new form.[1] This idea should remind you of Alfred Whitehead (who we looked at in Chapter 2) and his statement 'what is most fundamental about life is that it is motion' (rather than merely in motion).[2]

There will be, and will already have been, numerous times in your life where you go through intense change. Young adulthood and adolescence are certainly times when a lot of changes occur. Some of these intense changes are due to physical and hormonal changes, while others are due to changing situations, for example starting university or a new job. These changes have a profound impact on your development of who you are, and therefore can require a lot of consideration and restructuring of your perspectives and even your goals.

In this chapter, you are going to:

- explore who you might be in the future;

- consider the importance of your growth mindset and your creativity;

- take a look at the stages involved in the creative process;

- consider the relationship between resilience and creativity.

You have considered on numerous occasions throughout this workbook that who you are – your self and identity – appears and feels coherent and relatively stable over time, even while it is in constant development and motion. You have explored the role played by your personal identity in operating this dual feeling of stability and motion. You have also considered that your working self-concept or personal identity was the point where your past and your future communicated and came together. This, essentially, is where you can make meaning and sense of your past while preparing for your future; where you can imagine your future identities.

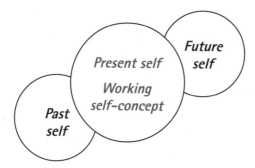

Recall that in Chapter 4, we considered how your present self in any given moment communicates to your future self about your past self. This facilitates the feelings of continuity and stability that we feel with regard to who we are.

Due to the feeling of continuity that we experience from our personal self and identity, we often underestimate how much we actually change, and *can* change.

Think back to what types of roles you played out as a child. You developed your imagination by imagining all sorts of roles and possible selves. You may have imagined roles such as being a:

- doctor, teacher, dancer, bus driver, farmer, musician . . .

Even at such a young age, you were already role-playing!

Make a list of the different roles you liked to play out as a child:

-
-
-
-
-

Which was your favourite role?

Have you decided to work towards fulfilling that role, or have you chosen something completely different?

Your growth mindset and creativity

In the previous chapter, you explored your identity growth in terms of failing forward and being comfortable making some mistakes. Here, you will explore your growth mindset in terms of your creative self.

Your growth mindset involves checking and correcting yourself instead of blaming others. It involves being responsible for your own behaviour and actions, and becoming empowered by being responsible for your own life.

> Beliefs about your creativity are an added dimension to your self and identity.
>
> *Creative self-efficacy*, like self-efficacy, is a belief in your ability, in this case your ability to be creative, and your personal judgement of your ability to come up with novel ideas and find creative solutions.
>
> How would you rate your creative self-efficacy?

> Evaluating your growth mindset

Take a moment and think about your growth mindset.

Read through the following statements and, for each item, select one of the response choices, and write the number for your choice in the space provided.

Remember to answer as honestly and accurately as you can.

1	2	3	4	5
Strongly disagree	Moderately disagree	Neither agree nor disagree	Moderately agree	Strongly agree

1. I generally take opportunities to grow as they come up _____

2. I actively work to improve myself _____

3. I am always trying to grow as a person _____

4. I believe that I can take steps to make positive changes in myself _____

5. I generally know when it's time to improve things about myself _____

Total score _____

Interpreting your results

5   10   15   20   25

Low
evaluation
of growth
mindset

High
evaluation
of growth
mindset

Reflecting on your evaluation

What have you learned about your evaluation of your growth mindset from filling out the self-questionnaire?

Is your evaluation high, moderate or low?

Are you surprised at how you evaluated your growth mindset?

Do you think you need to do more to improve your growth mindset?

Creative self-expression refers to your thoughts, feelings, ideas and emotions, which when not manifested verbally in interpersonal contexts are expressed through creative activity.

Creative self-expression is another useful way to improve your resilience. Creativity can be viewed as a resiliency mechanism to overcome stress and anxiety during difficult times.

The following is a list of creative behaviours, or behaviours of creative self-expression. Read through the list and tick which ones you have carried out in the past, or that you participate in frequently.

- Designed your own Christmas or birthday cards

- Knitted or crocheted something

- Created an original piece of music

- Wrote a song

- Learned how to play an instrument

- Made a cartoon strip

- Entered a science project into a competition

- Made a sculpture

- Wrote a story

- Made your own jewellery

- Wrote some jokes

- Made a film

- Made your own decorations

There are so many other expressions of creativity. Now try adding some past creative expressions of your own, or ones that you would like to do:

-

-

-

-

-

Creative expression through music offers a way to express your inner feelings in a creative outlet. Many musicians will describe how they use their music as a coping mechanism during difficult times. They often describe getting lost in the music as they can decentre and become part of the music.

Creative writing and poetry, and of course your journal entries in this workbook, can all offer channels for self-expression.

Future selves

In Chapter 4, you considered the role played by your social identity needs in guiding your conceptions of your future selves, in relation to focusing your attention. It was mentioned that your possible self or ideal or future self represents the set of traits, competencies and values you would like to possess. These are motivations towards who you might like to become, but also who you might fear becoming.

As images of desirable and undesirable end states, who you are is not just who you are right now or what you were like in the past, but also who you are striving to be. It is a concept of potentiality, of who you have the potential to be. Also call to mind the suggestion throughout this workbook of motion, and that you are not just dynamic, but uniquely dynamic.

Your hopes and dreams shed light on how you view yourself, as they express the type of person you want to become.

> Describe what type of person you would like to become.

> You have already carried out this activity in Chapter 4 – here, you have the opportunity to describe what type of person you would like to become and compare your descriptions.

Your ideal self is a guide to who you want to be, and is influenced by your social identity needs, your stored knowledge and your values. The self-work activities that you worked on in Chapter 2 are useful here in order to make judgements about whether your self-concept is compatible with your ideal self, and whether you are approaching your goal. All these self-work activities of metacognition, self-awareness and self-regulation are ready to be utilised from your psychological toolkit.

Using your newly acquired skills, try the next exercise:

Describe your true self in the present moment:

Describe your ideal self, who you are striving to become:

This is a great motivational tool to explore if there is a big or small discrepancy between who you are right now and who you want to become in the future.

Reflecting on your evaluation

How would you rate the distance between your present and future self? Is the distance close, or very far apart?

Are you surprised with how you have evaluated the distance, or is it how you expected?

Can you think of a plan to get closer to your ideal self? Perhaps this is already in motion.

The creative process

Creativity is a process of developing and expressing novel ideas that are likely to be useful. It is the creative act of developing new ideas about who you want to be in the future. Generating a new idea is only the beginning, not the end, of the creative process.

I would often tell my psychology students that novelty for its own sake is nothing more than an exercise in thought; that in order to be useful, we must push further and think of the practical significance of the idea.[3]

Creativity is the process of imaginative thinking (input) which produces new ideas, while innovations are the output. Karl Popper notes that there is no logical path leading to new ideas – they can only be reached by '*emfuhling*', i.e. creative intuition.[4] However, it is important to note that creativity is more than just dreaming up grand ideas, insights and problems; the solutions to these problems must be original and feasible.

Dorothy Leonard-Barton and Walter Swap, in *When Sparks Fly*,[5] propose five steps that capture the essential features of the creative process:

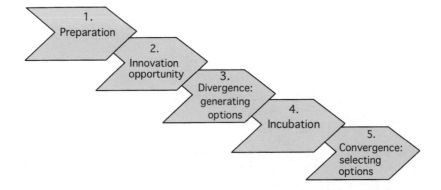

It will come as no surprise to you after all this self-work that creativity comes from a well-prepared mind, and so Stage 1 of the process is preparation. There also needs to be an opportunity for innovation to occur, which is Stage 2 of the creative process – for example, when it is time to try something new, or to make an improvement in a skill.

Stage 3 involves generating as many initial ideas as possible. This is divergent thinking, which involves considering as many different perspectives or developing as many different solutions as possible to a problem or difficulty that you want to overcome.

In this early idea-getting phase, you should not be too critical of initial ideas because premature criticism might destroy an emerging good idea. The old saying rings true here: you shouldn't throw the baby out with the bath water. During this phase, you can explore multiple alternatives of yourself.

Stage 4 involves incubation: the need for time out from struggling with an idea or issue, or just time to allow the idea to ferment; to get used to the idea. Finally, Stage 5 involves selecting an idea from your generated list of options. This is convergent thinking, and also involves combining elements in new, original and imaginative ways.

You can use this process to resolve any conflicts and contradictions that are having a negative impact on your wellbeing.

Summary

> **Fulfilment of social identity needs**
>
> **Affiliation:**   friendship and belonging
>
> **Autonomy:**   competence, control over decision-making
>
> **Esteem:**   social status and pride

> **Social identifications**
>
> • **Collective identification**
>
>   *Memberships*: school, college, class, family, peer groups, sporting groups, etc.
>
> • **Relational identification**
>
>   *Role Identities*: child, sibling, cousin, mother, musician, teacher, athlete, friend, etc.
>
> **Leading to multiple identifications and a flexible mindset**

Positive outcomes for self

Increased self-esteem and self-efficacy

Positive sense of self and wellbeing

Sense of belonging and acceptance

Emotional closeness, strengthened relational ties, liking and trust

Resilience, a compassionate mind

Feel safe to make mistakes and take risks

} Facilitates your ability to be CREATIVE

What have you added to your psychological toolkit?

- By now you are very clear that who you are is composed of a psychological entity that is both coherent and stable while also being in constant evolution and development. Creativity is such an essential resource in the construction of your identity and in your identity work.

- You can benefit greatly from a flexible mindset and from navigating through your multiple identifications in order to create a cognitive platform to be creative and to express yourself creatively. This can be achieved through the skills that you have in your psychological toolkit.

- Recall the different types of social identifications that you have constructed and developed in Part 2 of the workbook and their numerous positive benefits. For example, the close social connections and close relationships, teamwork and trust all create psychological safety which allows you to express yourself creatively without worrying about violations to your self-esteem.

11 My Mindful Self

Mindfulness, which Sylvia Boorstein has described as a balanced acceptance of the present experience,[1] has become such a popular concept today. Throughout the previous chapters, the focus has been on thinking on a deeper level about the self and identity, in meaning- and sense-making. We complement this process here by focusing on how you can mindfully self-regulate your attention and your immediate experience while you make sense of who you are.

Jon Kabat-Zinn, a medical doctor, has contributed greatly to the scientific application of mindfulness to help people cope with stress, anxiety, pain and illness. He is known for his mindfulness-based stress reduction (MBSR) programme. He describes mindfulness beautifully as 'the awareness that emerges through paying attention on purpose, in the present moment, and non-judgmentally to the unfolding of experience moment by moment'.[2]

In this chapter, you are going to:

- explore forgiveness, self-understanding and accurate perception;

- consider mindful meditation as a way of looking deeply into yourself;

- explore the importance of being mindful of social media and mobile phone use.

Mindfulness

Mindfulness involves self-regulation of attention to immediate experience and open acceptance of the experience. Remember your metacognitive skills. This allows you to produce higher levels of identity clarity, and to be truer to who you really want to be.

In Chapter 2, you also explored that at the very heart of metacognition, and in your self-work, you are aware of your subjective experience: how you are experiencing something. This can be described as your experiencing self.

It is deliberate non-judgemental attention, and involves focusing your attention, in a non-reactive way, to the thoughts and emotions that you experience. Non-reactive awareness refers to being more accepting, and less judgemental, and disregarding outside influences and your own biases. You are decentring in order to take a step back and observe the contents of your mind openly. This is an essential step in the metacognitive processes of monitoring, evaluating and regulating your thoughts and behaviours, as discussed in Chapter 2 and throughout the workbook.

Evaluating how mindful you can be

Take a moment and think about your own mindfulness.

We will consider three elements to mindfulness: awareness of thoughts and emotions; awareness of bodily sensations; and mind wandering. Read through the following statements and, for each item, select one of the response choices, and write the number for your choice in the space provided.

Remember to answer as honestly and accurately as you can.

Awareness of your thoughts and emotions

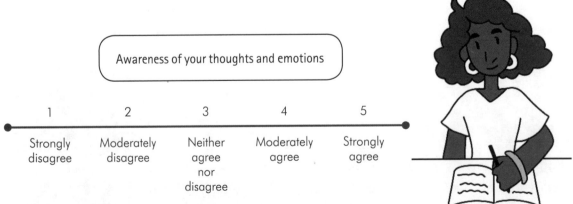

1	2	3	4	5
Strongly disagree	Moderately disagree	Neither agree nor disagree	Moderately agree	Strongly agree

1. When something upsetting happens, I take a step back and try to stay neutral while I make sense of the situation _____

2. I am able to perceive my feelings and emotions without having to react to them   _____

3. In stressful situations, I can pause without immediately reacting   _____

4. I find it easy to stay focused on what is happening in the present moment   _____

5. I pay attention to how my emotions affect my thoughts and behaviours   _____

Total score   _____

Interpreting your results

5	10	15	20	25

Low
awareness of
your thoughts
and emotions

High
awareness of
your thoughts
and emotions

Awareness of your bodily sensations

1	2	3	4	5
Strongly disagree	Moderately disagree	Neither agree nor disagree	Moderately agree	Strongly agree

1. When I'm walking somewhere, I like to deliberately notice the sensations of my body moving   _____

2. I like to pay attention to my sensations, such as the sun warming my face or the wind blowing through my hair   _____

3. I love to sit and listen to the sounds around me, such as the birds chirping or the traffic in the distance   _____

Total score   _____

Interpreting your results

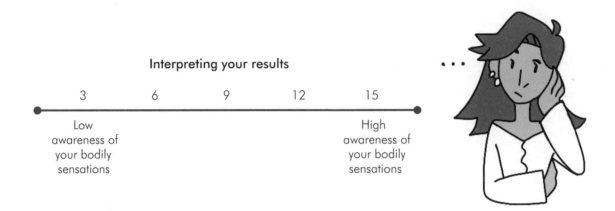

| 3 | 6 | 9 | 12 | 15 |

Low awareness of your bodily sensations

High awareness of your bodily sensations

Mind wandering

Your mind can wander when you are not engaged in purposeful activities, or when you are not focused on or engaged in the task that you are working on. The following traffic lane analogy is useful to illustrate this cognitive process: Once your mind is off the road (once your mind is off the present moment), you can easily wander or veer from the present lane (which is the lane that you should be working in), across lanes into your past worries or across further lanes into future challenges.

In *Positive Psychology and You*, psychologist Alan Carr describes the modern mind as a computer with too many files open. This slows down efficiency and makes your mind more likely to think of upsetting things and things that will make you anxious.[3]

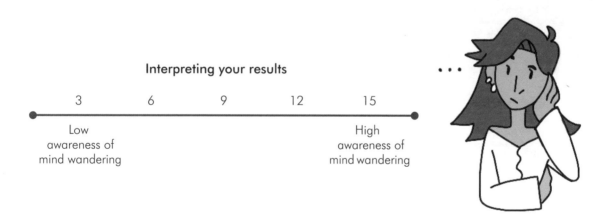

1	2	3	4	5
Strongly disagree	Moderately disagree	Neither agree nor disagree	Moderately agree	Strongly agree

1. I often do things without paying any attention _____

2. I often break or spill things because I am not paying attention _____

3. I get distracted easily _____

Total score _____

Interpreting your results

3	6	9	12	15
Low awareness of mind wandering				High awareness of mind wandering

Reflecting on your evaluations

What have you learned about your awareness of your thoughts and emotions from filling out the self-questionnaire?

Is your awareness high, moderate or low?

Are you surprised at how you evaluated your awareness?

What have you learned about your awareness of your bodily sensations from filling out the self-questionnaire?

Is your awareness high, moderate or low?

Are you surprised at how you evaluated your awareness?

What have you learned about your tendency to mind wander from filling out the self-questionnaire?

Is your tendency high, moderate or low?

Are you surprised at how you evaluated this tendency?

Is there anything you could do to improve your awareness of your bodily sensations or thoughts and emotions?

Mindful social media and mobile phone use:
Me, my mobile and I

My daughter got her first mobile phone in her first year of secondary school. Approaching the teenage years is often a time when young people get their first phone. Some people even get them at a younger age, depending on what is right for them.

Without careful planning and consideration, mobile phone use can affect your social interactions and communication skills, and you can become dependent on your phone.

Young people can become very attached to their phones, especially when they rely on text messaging as their primary way of communicating with their friends, which these days is the norm.

> Where is your mobile phone right now? (Is it in arm's reach?)
>
> Have you sent a text message or Snapchat message today?
>
> How many?
>
> Do you think you have become dependent on your mobile phone?

Nomophobia – No mobile **pho**ne pho**bia** – is the abbreviation for a modern-day phobia which has developed in young people due to their frequent interaction with new technologies; in this case, their personal mobile phones.[4] Nomophobia is the fear of being without your phone, and is a newly emerged psychological condition: the fear of being detached from your phone connectivity.

How has your life improved since owning a phone? How has it suffered?

Advantages of having a mobile/smartphone (with internet/Wi-Fi):

- You have constant communication and connection with others; you can send a message at any time, across time zones.

- You have unlimited access to unlimited resources of information.

- You can do so much on the go, for example send photos, have online lessons and talk to your friends.

- You can stay in touch with social networking.

Disadvantages of having a mobile phone:

- Security vulnerability; we store so much personal information on our phones, such as banking details, social security numbers, and so on.

- Dependence – we no longer know phone numbers off by heart, we rely so heavily on our phones. This can limit the performance of our memory and cognitive abilities. (Remember the importance of practice!)

- People's communication skills are declining, with fewer in-person, live interactions.

- Constant checking of your phone is a big distraction; it distracts you from the present moment and unfortunately leads to rude, anti-social behaviours such as not making eye contact or ignoring others altogether.

- You can rely on your phone too much, to the point of not being able to function without it.

- Your language and grammar can suffer due to so much texting in shorthand, and less time spent reading. This leads to incorrect spelling and grammar, and overreliance on abbreviations and text lingo. The use of emojis has become a language in itself.

- The constant pinging and beeping interrupts your mental flow and can be stressful.

Evaluating your mobile phone usage and how much you rely on it

Take a moment and think about your mobile phone use.

Read through the following statements and, for each item, select one of the response choices, and write the number for your choice in the space provided.

Remember to answer as honestly and accurately as you can.

1	2	3	4	5
Strongly disagree	Moderately disagree	Neither agree nor disagree	Moderately agree	Strongly agree

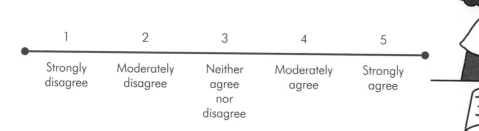

1. People say I spend too much time on my phone _____

2. I think about my phone a lot when I am not using it _____

3. I lose track of how much time I am using my phone _____

4. I sometimes continue to use my phone even when I have been asked to stop _____

5. The thought of not having my phone makes me anxious _____

6. I sometimes use my phone when I should be sleeping _____

7. When I stop using my phone, I get irritable and in a bad mood _____

8. I have ignored people because I have been using my phone _____

9. I have got into trouble at home, school or work because of my phone use _____

10. I have forgotten to do something because I lost track of time on my phone _____

Total score _____

Interpreting your results

10	20	30	40	50

Low
reliance
on phone

High
reliance
on phone

Reflecting on your evaluation

What have you learned about your reliance on your mobile phone from filling out the self-questionnaire?

Is your reliance on your mobile phone high, moderate or low?

Are you surprised at how you evaluated your reliance?

If you evaluated your reliance as high, what could you do to reduce your reliance on your mobile phone?

People tend to underestimate their mobile phone use. It is very important to be mindful of your usage. Apply your self-regulatory skills here and observe how much you use your phone for a day, then plan what you can do to decrease your usage if necessary.

Being mindful of what you share on social media

You can also benefit from being mindful and more aware of the motivations underlying what you share about yourself on social media. Mindful individuals are generally less self-conscious and less influenced by real and perceived responses to their self-presentations on Snapchat, TikTok, etc. You are less likely to become disappointed or upset due to how people react to what you share if you are mindful of social media self-presentations.

Young people today use social media and networking sites to communicate their identities by posting photos and writing self-descriptions. You will have the opportunity to explore your self-presentation and expressions through selfies on social media in Chapter 14.

> Self-compassion and self-kindness statements

The following are some simple and useful self-compassion and self-kindness statements. It is very beneficial to practise talking to yourself in this manner, and to remind yourself that you are not perfect, and that you are not supposed to be. What you are supposed to do for your positive wellbeing is to develop and become your truest self.

- I try to be kind to myself when I am going through a hard time.
- I try to be understanding with myself when I make a mistake or initially overreact; it is okay to make mistakes.
- When I notice things that I don't like about myself, I try to be understanding with myself, and plan how I can improve without being negative to myself.
- I will let go of worrying about what others think of me.

You explored similar ideas in Chapter 9 on resilience.

The statements above have been presented to you in quite a general format. The next self-work exercise gives you the opportunity to think more specifically about the ways that you can show yourself compassion and kindness.

It can be useful to think of a time when you were not kind to yourself, and construct a statement around how you could prevent yourself from thinking and behaving in that way to yourself in the future.

- _____

- _____

- _____

- _____

- _____

- _____

Summary

What have you added to your psychological toolkit?

Mindfulness techniques and exercises

There are numerous techniques and exercises you can carry out to become more mindful and also to reap the benefits that mindfulness has to offer. One such benefit is improving your concentration and your ability to keep information active in your mind, which of course involves your working memory, which you explored in Chapter 3. Here are some examples of mindfulness techniques:

- Yoga and stretching

- Mindful meditation

- Body scan exercises – Mark Williams, from Oxford University, has developed a very effective eight-week programme.[4] You can access his meditations and mindfulness resources on the following two websites:

  http://franticworld.com/free-meditations-from-mindfulness/

  https://www.oxfordmindfulness.org/learn-mindfulness/resources/

- Putting your body in charge – this can involve things like running up and down the stairs; going outside if you are inside; and standing up if you are sitting down. The idea is to distract yourself by allowing your emotions to follow your body, as opposed to the other way around.

- Mindful breath awareness meditation involves focusing on the sensations of your breath. For example, focus on the air flowing in and out of your nostrils. If any thoughts, feelings or other sensations arise, you should recognise them and then return to your breath without judging the distraction or giving it any more thought.

- As a form of brain network training, the brain networks that you are working are repeatedly activated and become stronger and more efficient.

12 My Grateful Self

Oliver Sacks was a world-famous neurologist and writer, and to my mind a psychologist. I am sure I made reference to him at some point in every module that I ever delivered to psychology students. He wrote some extraordinary books for the general public to help us understand the functioning of the brain. Probably his most famous book is *Awakenings*, which was adapted for film with Robin Williams playing a fictional neurologist based on Oliver Sacks himself who discovers a drug that helps catatonic patients, in particular a patient played by Robert De Niro.[1] Other noteworthy books of his are *The Anthropologist on Mars*, *The Man Who Mistook His Wife For a Hat* and *Seeing Voices*.[2]

During the final few months of his life, Sacks penned a beautiful book of essays, *Gratitude*.[3] Within these four essays, Sacks explores our wonderful uniqueness and the gratitude he experiences for the gift of his life.

In this chapter, you are going to:

- explore the importance of gratitude and the positive benefits for our sense of self and identity;

- develop a model of the stages involved in gratitude using your self-work skills;

- evaluate your own personal perceived level of gratitude;

- develop gratitude statements and carry out some effective gratitude activities.

What is gratitude?

Like many of the concepts that you have explored throughout this workbook, you already have an intuitive understanding of what *gratitude* is. It is a thankful appreciation for what you receive in life, whether it is gifts from other people or rewards you have worked for. It is a concept that has been written about extensively. For example, Melody Beattie proposed that gratitude unlocks the fullness of life, and turns what we have into enough and more,[4] while more recently, Barbara Fredrickson described how gratitude opens your heart and carries the urge to give back – to do something good in return, either for the person who helped you or for someone else.[5]

As with the self-work skills that you have developed, gratitude is another that involves intentional focus; you are deliberately being thankful. Mark Seligman and Robert Emmons (both pioneers of positive psychology), have researched the beneficial effects of gratitude and have found much to support the fact that it produces positive emotions and affect, and in turn has a positive effect on wellbeing. Gratitude helps you to feel more positive emotions, to focus on good experiences, and is associated with greater happiness.

Mark Seligman developed the well-known PERMA theory of wellbeing and happiness.[6] He is an advocate of the importance of studying what makes people happy; for him this is the most important research question that psychologists need to answer.

P – positive emotion. Your positive wellbeing depends on how often you experience positive emotions such as happiness, joy, pride and gratitude. In Part 2 of this workbook, we considered the positive affect for the self that arose from the fulfilment of our social identity needs. All that you have learned can be applied here.

E – engagement. Your positive wellbeing depends on how much you are involved in the tasks that you carry out. This produces intrinsic satisfaction in carrying out a task. This idea is similar to Mihaly Csikszentmihalyi's concept of *flow*. Flow, or being 'in the zone', involves the loss of self-consciousness and complete absorption in an activity.[7] Remember what we learned in Chapter 11 about living in the present moment and focusing entirely on the task at hand.

R – relationships. Recall in Chapter 6, we considered the importance of the social identity needs for friendship and belonging. All the positive resources of strengthened relationship ties, attachments, trust, feeling valued and seen, and psychological safety, are applicable here.

M – meaning. We have also considered in Chapter 7 the extent to which purpose in life, and having the autonomy to direct your behaviours and actions, is of value to you.

A – accomplishment. We have also considered the importance of accomplishment. We used the terms self-efficacy, self-esteem and pride in oneself. Recall that in enacting our roles well in relation to our relational identities, we are producing positive affect, which of course contributes to our positive wellbeing.

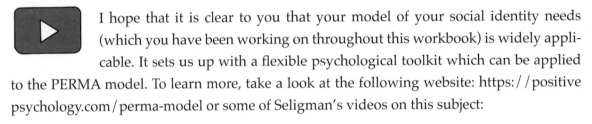 I hope that it is clear to you that your model of your social identity needs (which you have been working on throughout this workbook) is widely applicable. It sets us up with a flexible psychological toolkit which can be applied to the PERMA model. To learn more, take a look at the following website: https://positive psychology.com/perma-model or some of Seligman's videos on this subject:

- Martin Seligman & Positive Psychology – Pursuit-of-Happiness

- Positive Psychology in a Pandemic, with Martin Seligman, PhD

- #LarryKingNow with Martin Seligman: Grateful people are happier[8–10]

Three stages of gratitude

Robert Emmons proposed three stages of gratitude:

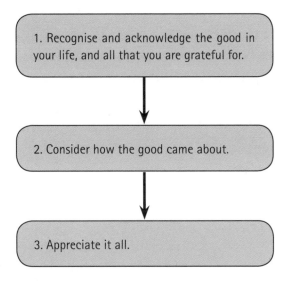

There are many TED Talks and YouTube videos that you can watch from the leading researchers in positive psychology, who focus a lot on gratitude. Robert Emmons has pioneered a lot of research and has developed some very useful theories, and Martin Seligman is another great thinker in the area. For a start, I would recommend these YouTube videos by Emmons and the Greater Good Science Center:

- Why Gratitude is Good

- Benefits of Gratitude

- The Power of Gratitude

- Cultivating Gratitude[11–14]

Now, try thinking of something that you have been grateful for recently, and apply your model of your metacognitive processes to it:

What have I been most grateful for recently?

5. *Planning*:

6. *Transforming*:

1. *Noticing*:

2. *Monitoring*:

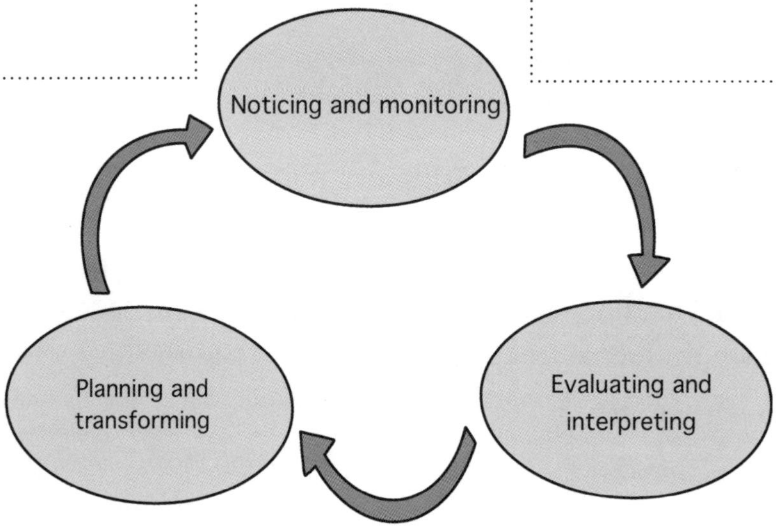

Noticing and monitoring

Planning and transforming

Evaluating and interpreting

3. *Evaluation*:

4. *Interpretation*:

Just like self-esteem in Chapter 8, gratitude can be a state or trait, and a self-evaluation.

- As a trait, you can practise gratitude as part of your daily life.

- As a state, this is an enduring personality characteristic. Not everyone feels grateful, so it is good news that you can practise gratitude and get better at it, and of course reap the psychological benefits of feeling grateful.

You will get to carry out some gratitude activities later in this chapter, which you can add to your psychological toolkit.

Evaluating your gratitude

Take a moment and think about what you are grateful for.

Read through the following statements and, for each item, select one of the response choices, and write the number for your choice in the space provided.

Remember to answer as honestly and accurately as you can.

1	2	3	4	5
Strongly disagree	Moderately disagree	Neither agree nor disagree	Moderately agree	Strongly agree

1. I am grateful for all that I have in my life   _____

2. I am content with who I am   _____

3. I do not compare what I have with others, I appreciate what I have   _____

4. I am grateful to everyone who has been a part of my life so far   _____

5. I am grateful to all of my friends   _____

6. Sometimes, I sit back and think of how grateful I am to be alive _____

7. I always try to appreciate the good and the bad _____

8. I have a long list of things to be grateful for _____

Total score _____

Interpreting your results

8   16   24   32   40

Low level
of gratitude
awareness

High level
of gratitude
awareness

Reflecting on your evaluation

What have you learned about your perception of your gratitude?

Is your level of gratitude high, moderate or low?

Are you surprised at how you evaluated your gratitude?

What more could you do to feel more gratitude?

Take a mindful moment and try some gratitude activities. You can practise these every day, or as much as you can fit into your daily life.

Fill in your own gratitude statements (prompts)

I am thankful for _____

_____

I appreciate that _____

_____

I value that _____

_____

I am grateful for _____

_____

What cheers you up after a hard day?

_____

_____

_____

What makes you feel loved, and why?

_____

_____

_____

What is something that money can't buy for which you are grateful?

_____

_____

_____

- Make your own deck of gratitude statements, using the prompts above to help you.

- Writing thank-you notes to friends and family helps you to get perspective on how they have helped or been kind to you. This elicits a lot of positive emotions in you, for example your feelings of belonging and being loved.

- Keeping a gratitude journal is another very useful tool for cultivating your gratitude. You can use the statements in the self-questionnaire that you have already completed and the prompts above to help you think and make sense of your own feelings of gratitude. Try to record at least three things each day for which you are grateful.

Gratitude journal

Date:

Today I am grateful for

_____

_____

_____

_____

_____

_____

_____

_____

_____

_____

_____

_____

_____

_____

Summary

What have you added to your psychological toolkit?

- In this chapter, you have considered how gratitude unlocks the fullness of your life, turns what you have into enough and elicits positive emotions in you.

- Feelings of gratitude towards others can increase social ties and connections with your friends, can decrease feelings of loneliness, and can facilitate a healthy mood and happiness.

- The reciprocation of gratitude among friends can offer emotional support, as when you connect with other people you feel seen, known, valued and (very importantly) understood. These feelings confirm your view of who you are; of your self and identity!

- The positive affect that arises from gratitude can also play a big role in building your self-esteem. Relishing and enjoying these good experiences improves your wellbeing and resilience, and also makes it easier for you to navigate through difficult times.

13 My Civic and Connected Self

Where does my mind stop, and the world begin?

The view of our self as social paves the way for such considerations as the question above. We are individuals with our own unique repertoire of personal identities, and we are also aware that our sense of identity extends well beyond our repertoire. We have looked at how we construct ourselves in roles, and as group members. Often these constructions have been in close proximity to us, for example our role within our family and at school or as a member of the local football team. In this chapter, we will look further afield in regard to our social identity constructions and look at our role in our communities, our countries and the world.

In Part 2 of this workbook, you looked very closely at the fulfilment of your social identity needs, and the numerous resources that were created through your social identifications. Psychological resources such as trust, emotional closeness, shared support, affection, positive regard for others and mutual understanding all strengthen your sense of connectedness with others. We will now look at how these positive outcomes can facilitate you becoming a good or even better citizen, and how these positive outcomes can motivate you to make decisions and act in ways that benefit your communities and the social environment at large.

In this chapter, you are going to:

- consider important pro-social and citizenship behaviours;

- explore your identification with your community;

- explore your identification with your country and the world;

- evaluate your civic and connected identity.

Pro-social and citizenship behaviours

> 'We must seek to build together an active inclusive citizenship; based on participation, equality, respect for all. . .' – Michael D. Higgins, President of Ireland, 2011[1]
>
> 'I am not an Athenian or a Greek, but a citizen of the world' – Socrates

Society benefits from engaged members who display *pro-social* and *citizenship behaviours*. These are extra role behaviours which are carried out for the good of those around you and for group members. In order to be an engaged member, they require that you identify with your community, your country or the world you live in.

Community and country citizenship behaviours

- Respecting others
- Being friendly to your neighbours
- Looking after the local and national environment
- Keeping your town and country clean and tidy
- Helping the vulnerable in society, e.g. the elderly

Can you think of any more behaviours to add to your list?

-
-
-
-
-

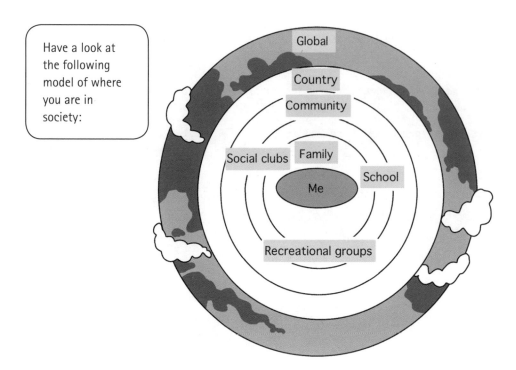

Have a look at the following model of where you are in society:

Identification with your community

Example: Repertoire of salient identities involved in the conception of a young mother's identity as a member of her community.

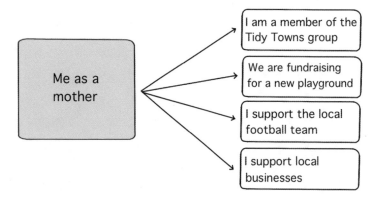

Example of an engaged community member

Fairy Friday: During the lockdown period of the COVID-19 pandemic, a lovely gentleman made fairy statues for our community. Every Friday, he would let us all know on the community Facebook page that the fairies were ready for collection. He set up a collection point outside his workshop, and each week the local children would come to get their fairies. Each week, he made a different mould to create a new fairy for the children to paint and collect. This brought great joy to the children, and created a sense of connectedness and community spirit in us all.

- We all felt gratitude towards him, and felt that we had a shared consensus and understanding of the importance of what he was doing for us.

- We also had a shared identity, as a group collecting these wonderful fairies.

Try constructing a model of your community identity for yourself. Think of yourself in terms of your roles and relationships, and your group memberships, within your community.

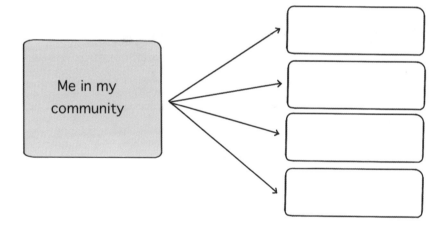

What kinds of activities could you engage in to feel part of your community? If you are already quite active, what else could you do?

How do you feel when you participate in community activities?

How does being a part of your community affect your self-esteem?

Are you grateful to be part of the community?

Identification with your national identity

Below are the identities I feel are salient in my conception of my national identity as an Irish person:

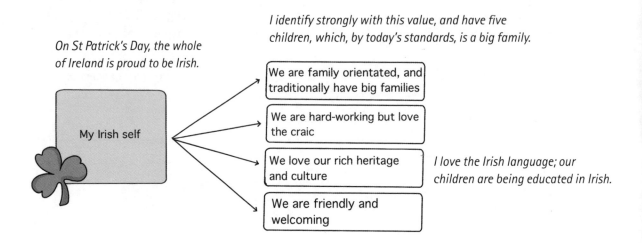

I identify strongly with this value, and have five children, which, by today's standards, is a big family.

On St Patrick's Day, the whole of Ireland is proud to be Irish.

My Irish self

> We are family orientated, and traditionally have big families

> We are hard-working but love the craic

> We love our rich heritage and culture

> We are friendly and welcoming

I love the Irish language; our children are being educated in Irish.

Try constructing your own model of your national identity. Remember to think of yourself in terms of your roles and relationships and your group memberships within your country.

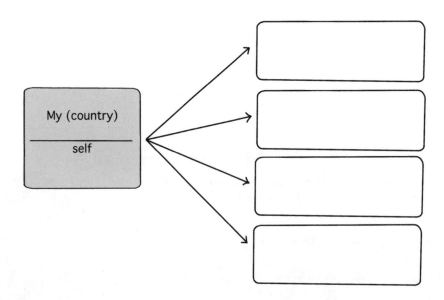

My (country)
_____
self

Are you proud to be a citizen of your country?

What is your country most famous/known for?

How does this affect your self-esteem?

Are you grateful for what your country has done for you?

What kinds of things could you do for your country?

'My fellow Americans: ask not what your country can do for you – ask what you can do for your country' – John F. Kennedy, 1961[2]

As well as being a citizen of your country, you are also a global citizen. You have rights and responsibilities as a citizen of the world, as well as within your country. I think your role as a global citizen develops as you get older. At a young age, you don't have a global perspective; this develops as you become concerned with what is happening in the world around you. You can widen and broaden your global perspective by actively keeping up to date with what is going on in the world.

Having a broader perspective of the world and of your role as a global citizen has numerous positive outcomes for your sense of self. For example, having empathy for those suffering due to war or natural disasters strengthens your sense of gratitude for what you personally have. You can also figure out ways you can help those less fortunate than you. For example, the Christmas Shoebox Appeal is a way that every person, young and old, can contribute to those less fortunate at Christmas. This involves creating shoeboxes full of toys, sweets and clothes which are sent to vulnerable children all over the world. Carrying out actions such as this will improve your sense of autonomy, friendship and self-esteem.

A global perspective also gives you a global anchor point for defining yourself, and gives you even more flexibility to navigate between and within your self-conceptions.

> Evaluating your civic and connected identity

Take a moment and think about your civic and connected identity. Your initial thought here may be that you can't articulate your identification with the larger environment. It may seem a bit too abstract.

Read through the following statements and, for each item, select one of the response choices, and write the number for your choice in the space provided.

Remember to answer as honestly and accurately as you can.

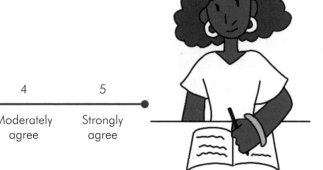

1	2	3	4	5
Strongly disagree	Moderately disagree	Neither agree nor disagree	Moderately agree	Strongly agree

1. It is important to me to feel part of the many generations of my family _____

2. Where I live and where I was raised are very important to me _____

3. I value my race and ethnic background _____

4. It is very important that I feel part of my community _____

5. I feel proud to be a citizen of my country _____

Total score _____

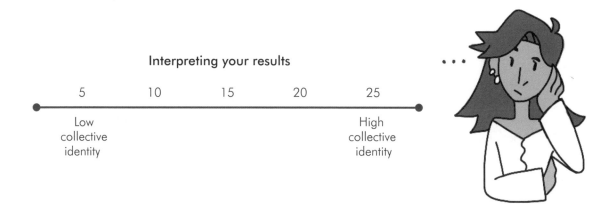

Interpreting your results

5	10	15	20	25

Low collective identity

High collective identity

What have you learned about your collective identity with your wider community and country?

Is the strength of your identification high, moderate or low?

Do you plan to do anything to increase how much you identify with your country and community?

Summary

What have you added to your psychological toolkit?

- The sense of connectedness which arises from your social identifications, both relational and collective, is so important in today's climate. It lubricates the social machinery of society. By this, I mean that the psychological resources gained by you act to promote social functioning in very positive ways.

- The positive affect that arises from social identification and social need fulfilment for the self (for who you are as a person) results in increased social capital. This involves strengthening the relationship ties (relational) and shared understanding (cognitive) of the collective, through social identity need fulfilment.

- The sense of belonging, connection, trust and gratitude all promote pro-social behaviours among members of communities, countries and the world as a whole. It promotes behaviours that go over and above roles for the common good.

- Identification with humanity facilitates compassionate behaviours and helps you to establish a self and identity that is balanced and not too self-focused or too other-focused.

14 My Self in the World Today

Social media use is widespread all over the world. Modern technology and social media have become a pervasive aspect of young people's daily lives, and as such have become a platform or context for creating who you are (your self and identity). Extending from the physical self that we considered earlier (in Chapters 1 and 8), we know that our physical appearance and self-esteem are often closely related.

In this chapter, you are going to:

- explore the significance of selfies as expressions of who you are;

- evaluate your online self-presentation usage;

- explore whether you are mindful of unrealistic presentations of people on social media;

- explore the use of avatars as a form of self-expression.

Self-presentation and expression through selfies

Self-presentation is a process of communicating one's own image to others. We have already considered that this only becomes psychologically real in relation to others. Technological self-expression is a new term for how young people present and develop their identities through technology, particularly by taking selfies and posting them to social networking sites. We looked at selfies briefly in Chapter 1, when we did some self-work about the physical self.

Taking selfies can act as a tool for exploring who you are (your self and identity) and can provide you with a visual diary of your life.

I like to use Facebook to share events with family and friends, and to look back on memories. For me, this also helps to satisfy my social identity needs for friendship and belonging. As a very busy mother of five, I use Facebook for a convenient quick fix, which eliminates the constraints of being unable to meet up with loved ones as much as I would like to in person.

Looking back at selfies that you have taken on your phone or that you have posted on Facebook can trigger self-study and self-observation. For example, you might wonder why you cut your hair a certain way, or why you always seem to wear a certain colour.

Have you ever looked back at your selfies and thought:

'Oh, I never realised I always did that in photos'?

In this way, selfies allow you to look back and consider your motives and actions, and gain more self-understanding. This is taking an internal perspective to your selfies; however, you may also take selfies with your public audience on Facebook or Instagram in mind.

From this outward perspective, selfies also act as a tool for how you construct and build up who you are, and allow you to try out multiple self-presentations of your self. This is a really useful way to try out new ideas of who you might want to be, to see if it feels like the real you. Remember Chapter 9, where we looked at the benefits of multiple identities for our resilience.

As a tool for self-promotion, you can post selfies to highlight your accomplishments and abilities. Providing that your posts are received well and the comments are positive, this certainly can fulfil your social identity needs for self-efficacy and self-esteem.

The *selfie paradox* is a term used to describe the idea that nobody seems to like selfies, or admit that they like them, yet everyone has a reason for taking them.

I believe the reluctance to admit liking selfies stems from a widespread shared judgement that it is superficial. But really we need to re-evaluate this judgement, as our physical identity is not a superficial element of who we are; it is integral to who we are. Our appearance and the way we express ourselves is how we choose to represent our identity visually.

That being said, I do believe that young people like yourself are far better at embracing selfies and self-presentation on social media than older generations.

> Evaluation of your online self-presentation usage

The purpose of the following questions is to help you evaluate how you feel about your online self-presentation usage.

Read through the following statements and, for each item, select one of the response choices, and write the number for your choice in the space provided.

Remember to answer as honestly and accurately as you can.

1	2	3	4	5
Strongly disagree	Moderately disagree	Neither agree nor disagree	Moderately agree	Strongly agree

1. I present many aspects of myself on social media   _____

2. I openly share my feelings and opinions in a sincere way on social media   _____

3. I post a variety of photos of myself on social media   _____

4. My self-presentations on social media are true reflections of who I am   _____

5. I present a comprehensive representation of myself on social media   _____

Total score   _____

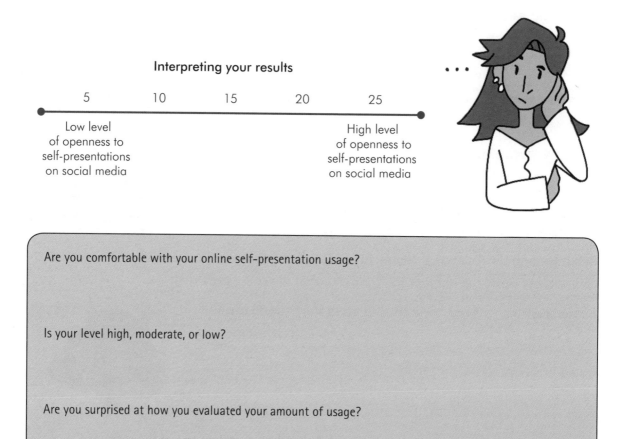

Interpreting your results

5   10   15   20   25

Low level
of openness to
self-presentations
on social media

High level
of openness to
self-presentations
on social media

Are you comfortable with your online self-presentation usage?

Is your level high, moderate, or low?

Are you surprised at how you evaluated your amount of usage?

Do you think you need to take any action?

Pressure to alter physical appearance and body image

Celebrity culture, complete with airbrushed images and apparently perfect lifestyles, is presented all over Facebook, Instagram, Snapchat, YouTube and TikTok. There is an unrealistic pressure for perfection, which is leading to growing anxieties about body image, especially where photos can receive a positive or negative rating.

This unfortunate social media pressure has had damaging effects on self-perception, and has led to an uptake in many types of cosmetic surgeries, some irreversible:

- dental veneers

- plastic surgery

- Botox

- dermal fillers

It is very disappointing to say that there are even makeover and plastic surgery apps aimed at young children, not just young adults and teenagers!

Be mindful of preoccupations with perfection

It is so important to always be mindful that this preoccupation with perfection leads to unrealistic expectations. The purpose of the following questions is to help you evaluate whether you have a realistic expectation or are preoccupied with perfection with regard to your selfies.

Read through the following statements and, for each item, select one of the response choices, and write the number for your choice in the space provided.

Remember to answer as honestly and accurately as you can.

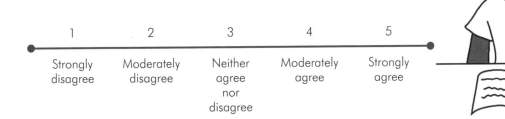

1	2	3	4	5
Strongly disagree	Moderately disagree	Neither agree nor disagree	Moderately agree	Strongly agree

1. I always have to look perfect   _____

2. If I appear perfect, people will like me more   _____

3.   I have to look like I always do things perfectly   _____

4.   I want to let everyone know when I do something well   _____

5.   I try to look perfect around other people   _____

6.   I do not want my friends to see any of my bad points   _____

Total score   _____

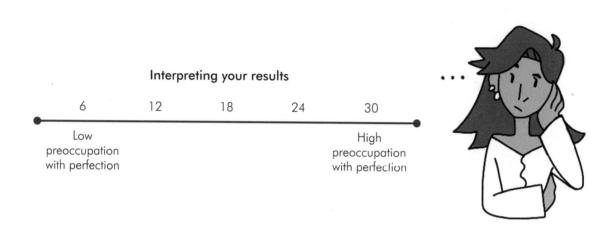

Interpreting your results

6   12   18   24   30

Low
preoccupation
with perfection

High
preoccupation
with perfection

> There is a beautiful Italian concept called *La Bella Figura* which is an approach
> to beauty that takes it to be far more than how you look: it is also how you
> carry yourself, how you interact and treat others, your manners and your grace.

Technological self-presentation and self-expression

Although we accept the evidence-based claim that self and identity reside in the frontal lobes of our brain (we explored this in Chapter 2), we will here consider the more recent claim that the mind does not exclusively reside in the brain or even the body, but extends into the physical world.

Objects in your external environment can become part of your cognitive processes and in that way they can function as extensions of your mind itself. This idea has been termed 'The Extended Mind Thesis' by Andy Clark and David Chalmers.[1] In Chapter 1, you explored how some parts of your personal identity could be determined by your external environment, for example your mobile phone, your laptop or iPad, even this workbook.

Avatars

For those of you who play video games, the following will be familiar to you. If you are like me and video games never appealed to you, this section may be new territory.

You can enter into video or online game territory by generating an avatar, which is a representation of you that could take the form of an animal or superhero, among many other things; this is your digital representation of yourself. It allows you to express yourself by selecting how to customise your character.

This has become really popular and is key for satisfying and immersive gameplay or online experiences. Avatars have become increasingly lifelike, and most games and online spaces now offer options for choosing your avatar, with some providing in-depth tools to modify every aspect of your digital representation.

You can also use an avatar to represent yourself on Facebook and Snapchat. There are websites that allow you to create your own avatar to share with your friends.

Identification with avatars can help with the fulfilment of many of your social identity needs, like social connection, self-expression, or identity exploration. However, it is important to be mindful of these questions:

- How much do you identify with your avatar?
- How much time do you spend in the gaming environment or on social media as your avatar?

When you create an avatar, do you create it to be:

- as realistic and similar to yourself as possible?
- an idealised version of yourself?
- distinctly different from yourself?

Summary

What have you added to your psychological toolkit?

- Considering the role played by advances in technology is crucial in developing a relevant conception of who you are.

- It is very important to apply your mindful approaches to your mobile and social media use. Just as it is beneficial to assess and evaluate your sense-making of who you are using your self-work tools, it is beneficial to apply them here in order to fully understand how your use of these technologies can impact on your mental wellbeing and your self-worth.

- Understanding how your view of your self extends beyond your body is very useful and gives you a more up to date and contextual view of how you act in your environment.

15 Concluding Comments

On completion of your journey

I hope that you have enjoyed this journey to learning about and coming to know your true self. I hope that you have found the development of your own positive theory and view of your unique self and identity to be enlightening and, most importantly, beneficial.

The first line that you read in the Welcome chapter was 'the way you think about yourself affects how you live your life!' Throughout *The Psychological Toolkit*, you have learned how you communicate with yourself and make meaning about yourself in a way that promotes your psychological health and wellbeing.

In order to reflect on what you have learned and the skills that you have developed, take a look at the following questions adapted from the Welcome chapter:

- Have you developed thinking skills and the necessary psychological tools and resources to develop and maintain your own positive sense of self and identity?

- Have you developed a strong understanding of your own self and identity, and your ongoing story of yourself?

- Have you improved your autonomy and ability to shape your own theory of self and identity, and taken power and ownership of your own thoughts, feelings and behaviours?

- Do you feel more in control of your wellbeing, resilience and mental health?

- Have you experienced an increase in your self-esteem?

- Do you understand your role in society, and how you can exhibit pro-social and citizenship behaviours in order to make a positive impact on the world you live in?

> • Have you connected more with your inner voice, and become your own personal advisor?
>
> • Have you become comfortable and fluent in using the psychological language of self and identity?

Some may answer yes to all or most of these questions, and some may not. You are all at different points on your unique journey. It may be beneficial to return to the exercise that you carried out at the beginning of the workbook, where you made an initial evaluation of your sense-making skills.

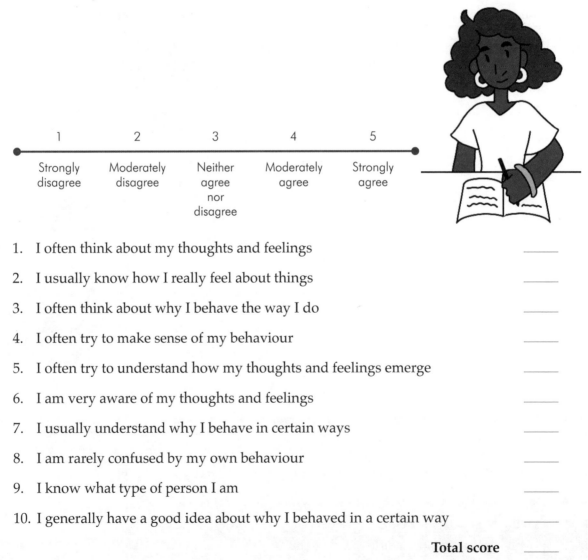

1	2	3	4	5
Strongly disagree	Moderately disagree	Neither agree nor disagree	Moderately agree	Strongly agree

1. I often think about my thoughts and feelings   _____

2. I usually know how I really feel about things   _____

3. I often think about why I behave the way I do   _____

4. I often try to make sense of my behaviour   _____

5. I often try to understand how my thoughts and feelings emerge   _____

6. I am very aware of my thoughts and feelings   _____

7. I usually understand why I behave in certain ways   _____

8. I am rarely confused by my own behaviour   _____

9. I know what type of person I am   _____

10. I generally have a good idea about why I behaved in a certain way   _____

                                                              Total score   _____

Interpreting your results

10	20	30	40	50

Low
evaluation
of your sense-
making skills

High
evaluation
of your sense-
making skills

· · ·

Compare your initial evaluation of your sense-making skills with your evaluation upon completion of
the workbook.

Have your sense-making skills improved?

Are you surprised by how much they have improved?

Do you think that there is more that you can do to improve your skills in the future?

I hope that you have experienced an improvement in your sense-making skills and that you
have developed an effective deep level of thinking about your self and identity.

As we have noted throughout the workbook, you are a work in progress, and you can return
to relevant chapters and exercises when you feel your psychological toolkit needs a boost
and some maintenance. Throughout the workbook, you have written records of your thesis
of your self and identity, and of what it means to be you; you have something tangible to
refer back to at any time. For example, you might answer the questions again in a few years,
and compare your two sets of answers to see how you have grown and developed.

In Chapter 5, you developed a model of your unique personal identity statements. Try constructing this model again, then compare it to your early model.

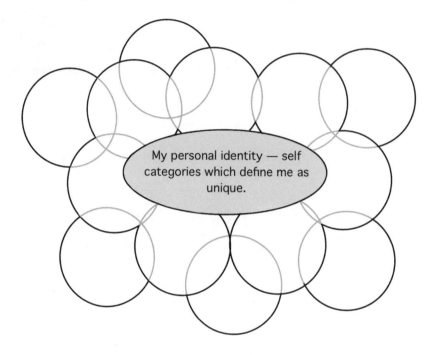

My personal identity — self categories which define me as unique.

Is your new model similar or different to your earlier model?

It is interesting to consider that changes in your identity statements may be highlighting the developmental nature of your self and identity – always in progressive motion.

Another interesting consideration is which identity statements have remained similar or the same? These represent the sense of continuity that we experience in our sense of self.

I think it is very useful to use this model from your psychological toolkit on numerous occasions throughout your life. There are benefits to looking back on your previous models, and also to constructing new ones.

If you are feeling a little lost, or completely lost, this will help you find your sense of self and identity, and your perspective.

We also considered the difficulty that can arise when trying to answer questions honestly, and in a way that is true to yourself. We noted how social influences from group memberships and roles, and perceived expectations from significant others, can all interfere with your authenticity as a person. I hope that as you have developed your self-work skills you have learned to be more mindful of these influences and feel able to process your feelings and actions in a beneficial way to your authentic self.

In Part 2, you developed your model of your social identity needs, which gave you a very useful tool for improving and maintaining a positive sense of self and wellbeing. All these new metacognitive skills and resources facilitate resilience, creativity, mindfulness and gratitude.

Social identity needs

Affiliation: Friendship
              Belonging

Autonomy: Competence
            Control over decision-making

Esteem: Social status and pride

Once a social identity need is activated or found wanting, you are then motivated to fulfil it.

motivating

Social identifications

- Collective identifications
  Memberships:

  School, college, class, family, peer groups, sporting groups, etc.

- Relational identifications
  Role Identities:

  Child, sibling, cousin, mother, musician, teacher, athlete, friend, etc.

Your social identity needs are fulfilled by your collective and relational identifications.

fulfilled

Positive outcomes for self

Self-esteem, self-efficacy

Positive sense of self and wellbeing
Sense of belonging and acceptance
Emotional closeness, strengthened relational ties, liking and trust
Resilience, compassionate mind
Safe to make mistakes and take risks

You gain positive outcomes from the fulfilment of your social identity needs.

My last word

As we considered at the beginning of the workbook, theories in psychology should be useful. The model that I have presented to you is evidence-based. I have tried to give you enough scientific research as I believed was needed to inform you of the relevant findings from psychology, but without toppling the balance towards something too theoretical. I hope that I have accomplished this.

My biggest motivation in writing this workbook is to equip young people with the skills and knowledge to apply psychology to their everyday lives. I wish you every success as you continue moving forward in your life with a psychological toolkit for a positive self and identity.

Acknowledgements

I would like to thank my husband Matt and our five amazing children, Clara, Maitiú, Oscar, Dáire and Rossa. Their love and support fuels my engine.

A big thank you to the editorial and production staff at Little, Brown Book Group. In particular, I would like to thank Andrew McAleer, who saw the potential and shared my vision to equip young people with the skill set to be proactive and positive about their self and identity. Your level of commitment and your high standards helped bring this book to life.

I would also like to thank Phoebe Munday; your illustrations connect and engage with young people in a creative and thought-provoking way.

Finally, I would like to thank all my students, clients and friends. For all the opportunities to communicate and interact, and to learn and identify.

Notes and References

Welcome

1. Elkhonon Goldberg (2001). *The Executive Brain: Frontal Lobes and the Civilized Mind*. New York: Oxford University Press.

2. Wing Shing Chan (2008). 'Psychological attachment, no-self and Chan Buddhist mind therapy'. *Journal of Contemporary Buddhism*, 9(2), 253–264.

3. Marvin Minsky (1986). *The Society of Mind*. New York: Simon & Schuster.

4. Jennifer Evans (2007). *Your Psychology Project: The Essential Guide*. London: Sage Publications Ltd.

5. Ernest Hemingway (1964). *A Moveable Feast*. New York: Scribner's (*A Moveable Feast: The Restored Edition* [2001]. London: Cornerstone).

6. Kurt Lewin (1951). *Field Theory in Social Science: Selected theoretical papers* (ed. Dorwin Cartwright). New York: Harper & Bros.

7. Ludwig Wittgenstein (1922). *The Tractatus Logico-Philosophicus*. New York: Harcourt, Brace & Co. Inc. and London: Kegan Paul, Trench, Trubner & Co. Originally published in German in 1921 as *Logisch-Philosophische Abhandlung* (Logical-Philosophical Treatise).

Chapter 2: What Does Self-Work involve?

1. Aldous Huxley (1932). *Texts and Pretexts*. London: Chatto & Windus.

2. Jerome Bruner (1990). *Acts of Meaning*. Cambridge, MA: Harvard University Press.

3. Jerome Bruner (1996). *The Culture of Education*. Cambridge, MA: Harvard University Press.

4. Jerome Bruner (2002). *Making Stories: Law, Literature, Life*. Cambridge, MA: Harvard University Press.

5. Robert Kegan (1982). *The Evolving Self: Problem and Process in Human Development.* Cambridge, MA: Harvard University Press.

6. Alfred North Whitehead (1929). *Process and Reality.* New York: Macmillan.

7. Carl Rogers (1951). *Client-Centered Therapy.* Boston: Houghton-Mifflin.

8. Elkhonon Goldberg (2001). *The Executive Brain: Frontal Lobes and the Civilized Mind.* New York: Oxford University Press.

9. René Descartes (1596–1650). *Principles of Philosophy,* covering his metaphysics and much of his natural philosophy (in Latin, 1644); *Treatise on Man* (in French, 1664), containing his physiology and mechanistic psychology.

10. Antonio Damasio (2006). *Descartes' Error: Emotion, Reason, and the Human Brain.* London: Vintage.

11. Frederick Tilney (1928). *The Brain: From Ape to Man.* New York: Hoeber.

12. Alexander Luria (1966). *Higher Cortical Functions in Man.* New York: Basic Books.

13. Alexander Luria (1982). *Language and Cognition.* Chichester: John Wiley.

14. Walle Jetze Harinx Nauta (1972). 'Neural associations of the frontal cortex'. *Acta Neurobiologiae Experimentalis,* 32, no. 2: 125–140.

15. Professor Noam Chomsky (8 April 2011). Lecture given at the Carlton University. *Language and the Cognitive Science Revolution(s).* YouTube: https://www.youtube.com/watch?v=XbjVMq0k3.

16. In 1907 William James published a series of lectures, *Pragmatism: A New Name for Some Old Ways of Thinking.* This was republished in 1995 by Dover Philosophical Classics, New York.

17. Aaron Beck (1967). *Depression: Clinical, experimental, and theoretical aspects,* New York: Harper & Row.

18. Tim Wilson & Dan Gilbert (2003). 'Affective forecasting'. *Advances in Experimental Social Psychology,* 35, 345–411.

19. Dan Gilbert – series of TED Talks on the surprising science of happiness and the psychology of the future self.

Chapter 3: The Remembering Self: My Self-Knowledge Memory Store

1. Tennessee Williams (1964). *The Milk Train Doesn't Stop Here Anymore*. Dramatists Play Service Inc.

2. Michael Gazzaniga, back cover quote from E. Tulving & I. M. Craik (eds) (2000). *The Oxford Handbook of Memory*. New York: Oxford University Press.

3. Richard Atkinson & Richard Shiffrin (1968). 'Human memory: A proposed system and its control processes'. In K. W. Spence & J. T. Spence, *The Psychology of Learning and Motivation* (vol. 2). New York: Academic Press, 89–195.

4. Fergus Craik & Robert Lockhart (1972). 'Levels of Processing: A framework for memory research'. *Journal of Verbal Learning and Verbal Behavior,* 11, 671–684.

5. Alan Baddeley & Graham Hitch (1974). 'Working memory'. In G. A. Bower (ed.), *The Psychology of Learning and Motivation: Advances in research and theory* (vol. 8). New York: Academic Press, 47–89.

6. Joseph LeDoux (1998). *The Emotional Brain*. London: Weidenfeld & Nicolson.

7. Alan Baddeley, 'The origins of the central executive': https://www.youtube.com/watch?v=aseitqCZKQo; 'On the development of the working memory model': https://www.youtube.com/watch?v=mT0NLihOK30; 'Introduction of the phonological loop': https://www.youtube.com/watch?v=2zF15C3vnIw; 'Introduction of the episodic buffer': https://www.youtube.com/watch?v=3a_cF46UiEU.

8. Richard Haier, 'Proof that *Tetris* makes you smarter' (2015): https://www.youtube.com/watch?v=oNudgqAK79s.

9. Susanne Jaeggi, Anja Pahor & Aaron Seitz (2022). https://socialsciences.nature.com/posts/who-benefits-from-brain-training.

10. Oscar Wilde (1895). *The Importance of Being Earnest, A Trivial Comedy for Serious People* was first performed on 14 February 1895 at the St James's Theatre in London. Numerous editions have been published, for example in 2005 by Prestwick House, London.

Chapter 4: My Motivating Social Identity Needs

1. William James (1890). *The Principles of Psychology*. New Edition (2000). New York: Dover Publications.

2. Abraham H. Maslow (1943). 'A theory of human motivation'. *Psychological Review*, 50(4), 370–396. https://doi.org/10.1037/h0054346.

3. Jacky Swan, Sue Newell, Harry Scarbrough & Donald Hislop (1999). 'Knowledge management and innovation: networks and networking'. *Journal of Knowledge Management*, 1367–3270.

4. Hazel Markus & Ziva Kunda (1986). 'Stability and malleability of the self-concept'. *Journal of Personality and Social Psychology*, 51(4), 858–866. https://doi.org/10.1037/0022-3514.51.4.858.

5. Charles Carver & Michael Scheier (1998). *On the Self-Regulation of Behavior.* Cambridge: Cambridge University Press.

6. Elanor Williams & Thomas Gilovich (2008). 'Do people really believe they are above average?' *Journal of Experimental Social Psychology*, 44(4), 1121–1128. https://doi.org/10.1016/j.jesp.2008.01.002.

7. Albert Bandura (1986). *Social Foundations of Thought and Action*. Upper Saddle River, NJ: Prentice Hall.

8. Carl Rogers (1951). *Client-Centered Therapy.* Boston: Houghton-Mifflin.

Chapter 5: My Psychological Resources of Social Identification

1. Paul Ricoeur (1962). 'The hermeneutics of symbols and philosophical reflection'. *International Philosophical Quarterly*, 2(2), 191–218.

2. Rom Harré (1993). *Social Being*. Oxford: Blackwell.

3. Carl Rogers (1951). *Client-Centered Therapy.* Boston: Houghton-Mifflin.

4. Edward E. Sampson (1993). 'Identity politics: Challenges to psychology's understanding'. *American Psychologist*, 48(12), 1219–1230. https://doi.org/10.1037/0003-066X.48.12.1219.

5. William James (1890). *The Principles of Psychology*. New Edition (2000). New York: Dover Publications.

6. Charles Horton Cooley (1902). *Human Nature and the Social Order*. New York: Scribner's.

7. Socrates (469–399 BC) was an ancient Greek philosopher.

8. Ciarán Benson (2001). *The Cultural Psychology of Self: Place, Morality and Art in Human Worlds*. London and New York: Routledge.

Chapter 6: My Need for Friendship and Belonging

1. John Bowlby (1969). *Attachment and Loss*. New York: Basic Books.

2. Abraham Maslow (1954). *Motivation and Personality*. New York: Evanston and London: Harper & Row Publishers.

3. Henry Murray (1938). *Explorations in Personality*. New York: Oxford University Press.

Chapter 7: My Need for Autonomy

1. Jean-Paul Sartre (1946). Lecture given in 1946, *L'existentialisme est un humanisme* (*Collection Pensées*), Paris: Nagel. Translated as *Existentialism is a Humanism* (2007). John Kulka (ed.), Carol Macomber (trans.), New Haven, CT: Yale University Press.

2. Richard De Charms (1968). *Personal Causation: The Internal Affective Determinants of Behavior*. New York: Academic Press.

3. Edward Deci & Richard Ryan (1985). *Intrinsic Motivation and Self-Determination in Human Behavior*. New York: Plenum.

4. 'Edward Deci – Self-Determination Theory': https://www.youtube.com/watch?v=m6fm1gt5YAM.

5. 'Intrinsic Motivation with Dr Edward Deci': https://www.youtube.com/watch?v=-Ba7bpEUONM.

Chapter 8: My Need for Self-Esteem

1. Edwin Locke, Kyle McClear & Don Knight (1996). 'Self-esteem and work'. *International Review of Industrial/Organizational Psychology*, 11, 1–32.

2. Viktor Gecas (1982). 'The self concept'. *Annual Review of Sociology*, 8, 1–33.

Chapter 9: My Resilient Self

1. Ernest Hemingway (1929). *A Farewell to Arms*. New York: Scribner. *A Farewell to Arms: Special Edition* (2013). London: Vintage Books.

2. The WCST was written by David A. Grant and Esta A. Berg. *The Professional Manual for the WCST* was written by Robert K. Heaton, Gordon J. Chelune, Jack L. Talley, Gary G. Kay & Glenn Curtiss. Free online version at https://www.psytoolkit.org/experiment-library/experiment_wcst.html.

Chapter 10: My Creative Self

1. Georg Wilhelm Friedrich Hegel (1807). *The Phenomenology of Spirit (The Phenomenology of Mind)*. There have been numerous translations and editions.

2. Alfred North Whitehead (1929). *Process and Reality*. New York: Macmillan.

3. Jennifer Evans (2007). *Your Psychology Project: The Essential Guide*. London: Sage Publications Ltd.

4. Karl R. Popper (1959). *The Logic of Scientific Discovery*. New York: Basic Books.

5. Dorothy Leonard-Barton & Walter C. Swap (1999). *When Sparks Fly: Igniting Creativity in Groups*. Cambridge, MA: Harvard Business Press.

Chapter 11: My Mindful Self

1. Sylvia Boorstein (1995). *It's Easier Than You Think: The Buddhist Way to Happiness*. San Francisco: Harper.

2. Jon Kabat-Zinn (2003). 'Mindfulness-based interventions in context: Past, present, and future'. *Clinical Psychology: Science and Practice*, 10(2), 144–156. https://doi.org/10.1093/clipsy.bpg016.

3. Alan Carr (2020). *Positive Psychology and You: A Self-Development Guide*. Abingdon: Routledge.

4. Venetia Notara, Elissavet Vagka, Charalampos Gnardellis, Areti Lagiou (2021). 'The Emerging Phenomenon of Nomophobia in Young Adults: A Systematic Review Study.' Addict Health 13(2); 120–136. https://dx.doi.orf/10.22122/ahj.v.13i2.309

5. Mark Williams. Body Scan exercises:
   http://franticworld.com/free-meditations-from-mindfulness/
   https://www.oxfordmindfulness.org/learn-mindfulness/resources/

Chapter 12: My Grateful Self

1. Oliver Sacks (1973). *Awakenings*. London: Picador; *Awakenings* (Dir: Penny Marshall, 1990).

2. Oliver Sacks (1995). *The Anthropologist on Mars*. London: Picador; Oliver Sacks (1985). *The Man who Mistook his Wife for a Hat*. London: Picador; Oliver Sacks (1991). *Seeing Voices*. London: Picador.

3. Oliver Sacks (2015). *Gratitude*. London: Picador.

4. Melody Beattie (1990). *The Language of Letting Go: Daily Meditations on Codependency*. Center City, MN: Hazelden Publishing.

5. Barbara Fredrickson (2009). *Positivity*. New York: Random House.

6. Melissa Madeson (2017). 'Seligman's PERMA+ Model Explained: A theory of wellbeing': https://positivepsychology.com/perma-model/.

7. Mihaly Csikszentmihalyi (1975). *Beyond Boredom and Anxiety*. Washington: Jossey-Bass Publishers. Find out more about 'flow' here: https://positivepsychology.com/what-is-flow/.

8. Martin Seligman & Positive Psychology – Pursuit-of-Happiness: https://www.pursuit-of-happiness.org/history-of-happiness/martin-seligman-psychology/.

9. 'Positive Psychology in a Pandemic, with Martin Seligman, PhD': https://www.youtube.com/watch?v=L1hauE_OKP8.

10. '#LarryKingNow with Martin Seligman: Grateful people are happier': https://www.youtube.com/watch?v=43zvL2b1oD4.

11. Robert Emmons (2010). 'Why Gratitude is Good', *Greater Good Magazine*: https://greatergood.berkeley.edu/article/item/why_gratitude_is_good.

12. 'Robert Emmons: Benefits of Gratitude': https://www.youtube.com/watch?v=RRrnfGf5aWE.

13. 'Robert Emmons: The Power of Gratitude': https://www.youtube.com/watch?v=jLjVOv
ZufNM.

14. 'Robert Emmons: Cultivating Gratitude': https://www.youtube.com/watch?v=8964env
Yh58.

Chapter 13: My Civic and Connected Self

1.   Michael D. Higgins, President of Ireland, Inaugural Address, November 2011. https://
president.ie/en/the-president/vision-for-presidency.

2.   John F. Kennedy, Inaugural Address, 1961. https://www.youtube.com/watch?v=
NwM6s55no6U.

Chapter 14: My Self in the World Today

1.   Andy Clark & David Chalmers (1998). 'The Extended Mind'. *Analysis*, 58(1), pp. 7–19.

OVERCOMING AVOIDANCE WORKBOOK

BREAK THE CYCLE OF
ISOLATION & AVOIDANT BEHAVIORS
TO RECLAIM YOUR LIFE FROM
ANXIETY, DEPRESSION, OR PTSD

DANIEL F. GROS, PHD

New Harbinger Publications, Inc.

Publisher's Note

This publication is designed to provide accurate and authoritative information in regard to the subject matter covered. It is sold with the understanding that the publisher is not engaged in rendering psychological, financial, legal, or other professional services. If expert assistance or counseling is needed, the services of a competent professional should be sought.

Distributed in Canada by Raincoast Books

Copyright © 2021 by Daniel Gros
         New Harbinger Publications, Inc.
         5674 Shattuck Avenue
         Oakland, CA 94609
         www.newharbinger.com

Cover design by Sara Christian

Acquired by Ryan Buresh

Edited by Kristi Hein

All Rights Reserved

Library of Congress Cataloging-in-Publication Data on file

Printed in the United States of America

23   22   21

10 9 8 7 6 5 4 3 2 1   First Printing